THE LITTLE BOOK OF LORE FOR

CAT LOVERS

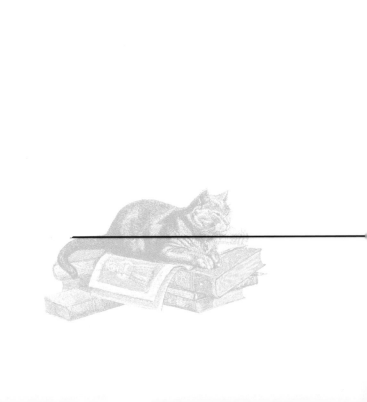

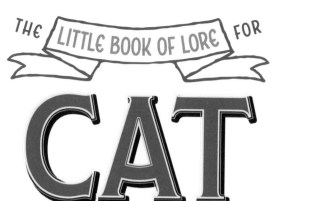

THE LITTLE BOOK OF LORE FOR

CAT LOVERS

A COMPLETE CURIOSITY OF FELINE FACTS, MYTHS, AND HISTORY

DEBORAH ROBERTSON

Skyhorse Publishing

First Skyhorse Publishing edition
© Toucan Books Ltd. 2021

Skyhorse Publishing books may be purchased in bulk at special discounts for sales promotion, corporate gifts, fund-raising, or educational purposes. Special editions can also be created to specifications. For details, contact the Special Sales Department, Skyhorse Publishing, 307 West 36th Street, 11th Floor, New York, NY 10018 or info@skyhorsepublishing.com.

Skyhorse® and Skyhorse Publishing® are registered trademarks of Skyhorse Publishing, Inc.®, a Delaware corporation.

Visit our website at www.skyhorsepublishing.com.

10 9 8 7 6 5 4 3 2

Library of Congress Cataloging-in-Publication Data is available on file.

Cover design by Daniel Brount
Cover illustration from Getty images

Print ISBN: 978-1-5107-6291-6
Ebook ISBN: 978-1-5107-6292-3

Printed in China

CONTENTS

CHAPTER 1

Understanding Cats

Pet cats are amazingly adept at occupying two seemingly parallel

universes. Within one neat furry package there coexists a

well-armed, ruthless nocturnal hunter and a beguiling,

manipulative, purring cat. One can terrorize the local rodent and

bird populations; the other can wrap you around its long tail and

knows all the right buttons to push and heartstrings to tug to live

a life of cosseted luxury. Being able to read your cat's body

language and interpret its meowing simply means you can

anticipate its mood and desires more swiftly and accurately.

WHERE CATS COME FROM

Today's domestic cats are probably all descended from the wildcat *Felis silvestris lybica*, a species native to the Middle East. It's estimated that there may now be half a billion domestic cats around the world, at a time when the existence of the other 36 or so species of wildcat is threatened or endangered.

The cat has followed humans for about 10,000 years, tagging along from primitive farming communities to the urban jungle. The earliest example of a domestic cat was found in a Neolithic grave on Cyprus, among the dead of people who probably brought the animal from Turkey. It has been dated to about 7500 B.C., which links to the origins of agriculture. By about 2000 B.C., when the Egyptians realized how useful the cat was in protecting their grain (see page 64), they had invited the cat into their homes—or, more likely, the cat adopting the humans instead of the humans adopting the cat.

Two ratters given to a Huron Indian chief might have been the first cats in North America. Sadly, they died without producing kittens. Some think the domestic cat arrived on the *Mayflower*. In 1749, cats were imported from England to control the rats.

> *The cat, it is well to remember, remains the friend of man because it pleases him to do so and not because he must.*
>
> CARL VAN VECHTEN (1880–1964)
> AMERICAN WRITER AND PHOTOGRAPHER

TOP TEN COUNTRIES WITH THE MOST PET CATS

One unofficial estimate puts the total cat population in the United States at around 93 million, based on 63 million pet cats and about 30 million feral cats—ferals are the wild offspring of domestic cats, which by definition are hard to count. Some people feel that this is a gross underestimation and would guestimate that there could be one feral for every pet cat in the country. Cats have overtaken dogs as the most popular pet in the United States.

COUNTRY	NUMBER OF CATS
United States	76,430,000
China	53,100,000
Russia	12,700,000
Brazil	12,466,000
France	9,600,000
Italy	9,400,000
Great Britain	7,700,000
Ukraine	7,350,000
Japan	7,300,000
Germany	7,200,000

POPULATION EXPLOSION

If left to her own devices, a female cat can have three to seven kittens every four months. Theoretically, in five years, one un-neutered female cat can have over 20,000 descendants. One pair of breeding cats and their offspring can produce over 400,000 new cats in seven years. Unlike humans, female cats do not have a menopause and remain fertile throughout their lives, unless neutered.

A cat called Dusty, living in Bonham, Texas, was 17 years old when she gave birth to her 420th kitten on June 23, 1952.

In 1987, a cat called Kitty, owned by George Johnstone of Croxton, Staffordshire, England, produced a litter of two kittens—at the magnificent age of 30! Kitty died 2 years later, at the age of 32.

One in four pregnant cats carries kittens fathered by more than one mate. A fertile female may mate with several tomcats, which fertilize different eggs each time, which is why kittens in the same litter can have different colors and coats.

> *No matter how much cats fight,*
> *there always seems to be plenty of kittens.*
>
> ABRAHAM LINCOLN (1809–65),
> 16TH PRESIDENT OF THE UNITED STATES

A sexually active feral tomcat lays claim to an area of about 3 square miles (8 sq km) and sprays strategic points with strong smelling urine to mark his territory. Most cats killed on the road are un-neutered toms, because they are more likely to roam farther afield and cross busy roads.

Global warming is blamed for many environmental problems, and now it seems as though it's also responsible for a feline population explosion. As the winters become shorter and milder, cats start breeding earlier and there is less of a lull in kitten production.

THE AGING CAT

Cats, like people, are living longer than ever. Here's a comparison of how a cat ages in comparison to a human. Of course, also like people, cats age at different rates, depending on their genes and environmental factors.

CAT'S AGE	EQUIVALENT HUMAN AGE	COMPARISONS
2–3 months	9–12 months	Weaned and becoming more independent.
4 months	2–3 years	Children mobile and talking; kittens completely independent of mother.
6–12 months	12–15 years	Kitten and adolescent are both sexually mature but may still be growing.
2 years	24 years	Completely independent—if your lucky.
3–6 years	28–40 years	Human career and family building.
6–9 years	40–52 years	Creeping middle-age spread; some women have already entered menopause.
9–13 years	52–65 years	Retirement looms; cats begin to slow down, too.
13–17 years	65–85 years	Still active but getting older: less agile mentally and physically; injuries heal more slowly; internal organs less efficient.
17–19 years	83–92 years	Increasingly frail: hearing, sight, and mobility deteriorating; bones thinning; less fat; delicate skin; less supple; weaker muscle tone.
19–22 years	92–100 years	Declining years.
22+ years	100+ years	More and more cats and humans are reaching this venerable age.
30 years	136 years	Now cats outstrip humans; several have reached this age.
34–36 years	152–160 years	Officially oldest cat. According to Guinness World Records, the oldest cat was Creme Puff, who lived to 37; he belonged to Jake Perry of Austin, Texas.
43 years	188 years	Unverified cat claim.

ANATOMICAL FACTS

The cat has a reflective tissue at the back of its eyes to increase the light reaching the retina—this is also what makes a cat's eyes glow in the dark. Contrary to popular belief, cats cannot see in total darkness.

A cat's hearing ability is five times that of a human. A dog has a greater range of pitch, but a cat's hearing exceeds a dog's for high-pitched sounds, such as the squeak of a mouse. Cats can and do hear ultrasonic sounds that precede a noisy event, such as an earthquake or storm.

Although a cat's sense of smell is much better than a human's, it's not as developed as a dog's. However, it is fully developed at birth, and a kitten can tell the difference between its mother's nipples and those of another cat by their smell.

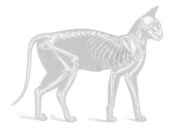

All of an adult cat's 30 teeth are designed to shred meat—instead of chewing food, they chop it. The large canines, or fangs, are used to break the necks of their prey. It's reckoned that cats are responsible for killing 566 million birds each year.

A cat's whiskers are basically thick hairs with well-developed sensory organs. Each side of the cat's nose has a set of 12 whiskers, which are normally as long as the widest part of the cat's body—unless it is obese or pregnant. The whiskers can detect nearby movement, which is handy when hunting in the dark.

Just like humans are often left-handed or right-handed, cats have a preferred front paw. Only 20 percent are right-pawed, while 40 percent are left-pawed and the remaining 40 percent are ambidextrous.

There is no firm consensus on the mechanism of the purr. Some say it originates in the larynx (voice box) when a second pair of vocal chords start vibrating; others believe it is generated by blood flow resonating in the wind pipe and nasal cavities.

FURRY FRIENDS

 Most cats have true fur, which means they have both a soft, fine undercoat and a long, coarser outer coat. A cat sheds its fur when it spends more time in light—which is why an outdoors cat sheds its coat in spring, when there is more daylight, until fall, when daylight is shorter. House cats also shed because of exposure to light from lightbulbs and even appliances, such as the television.

A nerve is connected to each hair in a cat's coat. When stroked, there is a decrease in the cat's muscle tension and heart rate—which is, funnily enough, what also happens to the person stroking the cat.

If you sneeze whenever you're around cats, it's probably not the cat hair that irritates your nose, but the saliva that remains on their fur. Cat saliva contains a detergent that keeps their fur clean. While this is great for the cat, it isn't for people who are allergic to cats. If the resident cat is bathed and groomed regularly, allergic people can sometimes tolerate it better.

Studies now show that the allergen in cats is also related to their scent glands. Cats have scent glands on their faces and at the bottom of their tails. Un-neutered male cats generate the most scent. If this secretion from the scent glands is the allergen, allergic people should tolerate spayed female cats the best.

THE TABBY

The tabby is not a distinct breed of cat but a coat pattern that can appear in all breeds. It most closely resembles the pattern on the cat's wild ancestor. The word "tabby" stems from *attabi*, which describes the swirling markings on silk fabrics woven in the Attabiya district of Baghdad in Iraq.

CLASSIC OR BLOTCHED TABBY has bold, swirling patterns of dark and lighter circular smudges arranged like a bull's-eye on its sides.

MACKEREL TABBY, sometimes known as a tiger cat, has narrow parallel stripes down the sides of its body. The best stripes are evenly spaced, unbroken lines that branch from one stripe running along the spine like a fish skeleton, which is why the pattern is described as mackerel.

TICKED TABBY, sometimes called an Abyssinian or agouti tabby, doesn't have any traditional stripes or spots on its body, so it doesn't look much like a tabby. However, its coat has tabby markings on the face and agouti hairs on the body. Agouti hairs are best seen in the lighter parts of a tabby's coat, where you'll see that the individual hairs are striped with alternating light and dark bands.

SPOTTED TABBY has spots all over its sides. They may be large or small, round, oval, or rosette, and they sometimes appear to be broken mackerel stripes. A mackerel tabby with a broken stripe pattern can look a lot like a spotted tabby.

PATCHED TABBY is used to describe a tortoiseshell tabby. Typically, the cat's coat has separate patches of brown tabby and red tabby. A tortoiseshell carrying the tabby gene is often called a tortie. Patched tabbies can show any of the four distinct tabby patterns. The markings are usually more apparent on the legs and head.

A COAT OF MANY COLORS

An orange cat may be just an orange cat to most people, but to cat breeders its coat is red, to children's story writers, it's marmalade, to British people it's ginger, and, in the old days, it would have been called yellow.

The gene in cats that causes the orange coat color is sex linked, and carried on the X sex chromosome. This gene may show itself as orange or black. A male cat, with only one X chromosome, can be only orange or black, but not both. A female cat with two X chromosomes may have both orange and black colors in its coat, which is why almost all tortoiseshell cats are female.

It is extremely rare to come across a male cat with both orange and black in his coat. To have both the orange and the black coat colors, the male cat must have all or part of both female X chromosomes. This unusual sex chromosome combination would make him sterile.

When a six-month-old tortoiseshell stray was brought into the Escondido Humane Society in San Diego, California, to be spayed, the veterinarian was shocked. Phinny—short for Phenomenon, as the cat became known—turned out to need neutering because "she" was a "he." Male torties are rarely seen and Phinny was a genuine genetic anomaly.

WHITE MARKINGS

A cat that has . . .	is said to be/have . . .
white paws	mitted
a white patch on its chest	a locket cat
small white patches on its belly	buttons
a roughly half-white coat	bicolor
a mostly white coat with a few color patches	harlequin
a black coat with white legs, underside, and chest	a tuxedo cat
a black-and-white coat	a jellicle cat

BODY LANGUAGE

A relaxed cat arches its back to stretch sleepy muscles after a nap. However, an arched back, with hair standing on end all over its body, especially its tail, conveys that it's feeling threatened. Turning sideways on presents an even more impressive profile to scare away a threat.

TAIL SHAPE AND POSITION	MOOD
Curves down, then up at the tip	Content and peaceful
Slightly raised and gently curved	Curious and interested
Vertical with tip tilting over	Friendly and interested, but cautious
Vertical with tip stiffly upright	Happy and unreservedly welcoming
Vertical and quivering	After greeting, a friendly "Hi!"
Lowered or between legs	Submissive and subdued
Low and puffed out	Fearful
Arched and bristling	Defensive
Straight and bristling	Aggressive
Still, but tip twitching	Irritated—the more twitching, the greater the irritation
Swishing from side to side	Angry conflict; attack imminent
Held to one side	Female inviting male to mate

POSITION OF EARS	MOOD
Facing forward, tilted slightly back	Happy and relaxed
More pricked	Alert; if they begin to twitch or turn, feeling slightly anxious or uncertain
Nervously twitching	Agitated, suggesting conflict, frustration, or apprehension
Fully flattened	Defensive; also a practical measure to protect the ears if a fight ensues
Swiveled but not fully flattened, with backs visible from front	Aggressive—clearest warning of imminent attack a cat can convey

CAT CALLS

A domestic cat develops a part of its vocabulary to appeal to people and a part to communicate with other cats.

SOUND	MEANING
In a standoff or fight, a cat starts caterwauling; it delivers a barrage of growls, snarls, wails, and howls.	I'm angry.
Throaty howl when cornered	I'm frightened.
Hissing, accompanied by spitting	Stand back! Because it sounds like a snake, most animals withdraw.
Scream in cat or squeal in kitten	I'm in agony.
Meow, variable in duration and volume	A multitude of messages that usually mean "Pay attention to me—now!"
Gentle chirruping	Used by a mother cat to encourage her kittens to follow her, but retained in domestic cats as a greeting.
Purring—a soft rumbling rolling *rrrrrrr* that is one of the most seductive sounds in the world	Purring performs many purposes. As a sign of friendship it helps to establish a bond between mother and kittens, breaks down social barriers, and defuses potential conflict. Cats also purr when they're injured, frightened, or giving birth, possibly because the vibrations of purring serve a mechanical function in reducing pain and speeding up healing.
Teeth chattering	Heard when a hunting cat spots its prey and is fully focused on it.

 Her purrs and mews so evenly kept time.
JOHN WINSTANLEY (c. 1677–1750), IRISH POET

CHAPTER 2

Cats of the Famous & Rich

The masters of chill out, cats are the perfect antidote to the hurly-burly of fame and fortune. For centuries, there have been cats curling up on the laps of powerful leaders or draping themselves around the shoulders of authors and composers. As a nonjudgmental companion, many a beloved cat has provided a welcome distraction from the trials and tribulations of governing a country, waging wars, writing a blockbuster, composing a masterpiece, or performing on screen.

FAMOUS WRITERS
AND THEIR CATS

OWNER	OCCUPATION	CAT
Brian Aldiss (1925–2017)	English science-fiction novelist	Foxie, Jackson, Macramé, Nickie, Yum-Yum
Sir Kingsley Amis (1922–95)	English author	Sarah Snow
Jorge Luis Borges (1899–1986)	Argentinian writer	Beppo
Charlotte Brontë (1816–55)	English novelist	Tiger
Emily Brontë (1818–48)	English novelist	Tiger
Helen Gurley Brown (1922–2012)	Editor	Samantha
Lord Byron (1788–1824)	English poet	Beppo
Cecil Day-Lewis (1904–72)	Irish poet	Simpkin
T. S. Eliot (1888–1965)	American poet	Tantomile, Wiscus
F. Scott Fitzgerald (1896–1940)	American author	Chopin
Paul Gallico (1897–1976)	American author	Chilla and Chin
Théophile Gautier (1811–72)	French poet/novelist	Zizi
Thomas Hardy (1840–1928)	English novelist	Cobby
Ernest Hemingway (1899–1961)	American writer	Thruster
Victor Hugo (1802–85)	French writer	Chanoine, Gavroche, Mouche
Dame Iris Murdoch (1919–99)	Irish writer	General Butchkin
Gabriele Rossetti (1783–1854)	Italian poet	Zoe
Georges Sand (1804–76)	French novelist	Minou
Dorothy L. Sayers (1893–1957)	English detective story writer	Timothy
William Makepeace Thackeray (1811–63)	English author	Louisa
H. G. Wells (1866–1946)	English science-fiction writer	Mr. Peter Wells
Ella Wheeler Wilcox (1850–1919)	American author/poet	Ajax, Banjo, Goody Two Eyes, and Madame Ref
Tennessee Williams (1911–83)	American playwright	Topaz

THE MUSE
THAT MEOWED

Ailurophilia is a serious condition that afflicts many people, including the famous and rich. The main symptoms manifest themselves as an often soppy devotion to cats.

Dr. Samuel Johnson (1709–84), the compiler of the first comprehensive dictionary of the English language, doted on his cat Hodge so much that he went into town himself to buy oysters and feed them to his overindulged cat personally. Visitors to London, England, can find Hodge—or at least a gleaming bronze statue of him—sitting on a copy of the original dictionary, surrounded by shucked oyster shells, opposite Number 17 Gough Square, near Fleet Street, where he and Dr. Johnson once resided.

Edward Lear (1812–88), the talented illustrator and writer of nonsense verse, drew his beloved tabby cat, Foss, many times. It is believed that Foss inspired him to write his classic poem, "The Owl & the Pussycat." When Lear was having a new house built in San Remo, Italy, it is thought he had it built to exactly the same layout as his previous home so that Foss would settle down in his new home immediately. When Foss died, Lear buried his much-loved feline companion in his garden. He survived his cat by only two months.

Hinse, a huge tomcat belonging to Sir Walter Scott (1771–1832), terrorized Scott's dogs until, one day, a bloodhound named Nimrod took his revenge and killed him in 1826.

MORE MEOWING MUSES

🐾 Edgar Allan Poe (1809–49) adored his tortoiseshell cat, Catarina, who often got a shoulder's eye view of the famous author's work. In fact, Catarina inspired Poe to write one of his most well-known tales, *The Black Cat*. Unfortunately, when Poe's wife, Virginia, lay dying of consumption, Poe was too poverty stricken to heat her room. However, Catarina came to the rescue—Poe placed the feline on the bed to keep his wife warm.

🐾 After the death of his prescient cat, Mysouff I, Alexandre Dumas (1802–70), the French novelist, adopted a black-and-white cat that his cook found, and he called it Mysouff II (see page 90). The new Mysouff was soon a favorite until one day it ate all the exotic birds in Dumas's aviary. At the cat's trial, it was pointed out by the counsel for the defense that Mysouff II had only been able to gain access to the aviary because the door had been opened by Dumas's pet monkeys. Sentencing the poor cat to spend five years in the monkey's cage was deemed to be a fitting punishment for its heinous crime. As luck would have it, shortly afterward, Dumas fell on hard times and had to sell his mischievous monkeys, reprieving the naughty Mysouff II.

🐾 Another famous French writer, Victor Hugo (1802–85), who penned such classics as *The Hunchback of Notre Dame* and *Les Misérables,* also adored cats and wrote about them in his diaries.

Harriet Beecher Stowe (1811–96), author of *Uncle Tom's Cabin*, loved a large Maltese cat called Calvin. (Just to confuse matters in the Stow household, her husband's name was Calvin, too.) The cat just turned up on Harriet's doorstep one day, moved in, and took over her heart. He would often sit on her shoulder as she wrote and Harriet enjoyed his company.

Apparently Mark Twain, the pen name of Samuel Langhorne Clemens (1835–1910), always chose convoluted names for his many cats—Apollinaris, Beelzebub, Blatherskite, Buffalo Bill, Tammany, and Zoroaster are only six of them—to help his young children learn how to pronounce multisyllabic words.

The author Charles Dickens (1812–70) had a white cat called William— until "William" had kittens and became Williamina. The kittens were born in the kitchen, and there they were meant to stay, except Williamina kept carrying them into Dicken's study. Inevitably, the mother cat got her way and the little cats grew up beside the author as he wrote. He must have grown fond of them because he kept one of the kittens, which became known as The Master's Cat.

The American author Raymond Chandler (1888–1959), writer of the Philip Marlowe detective books, used to talk to his cat, Taki, who sat on his manuscripts as he worked on them.

The American writer and journalist Ernest Hemingway (1899–1961), winner of both the Pulitzer Prize and Nobel Prize, was a huge cat lover—in fact, he owned 30 cats. The first of these cats, given to him by a ship's captain, was polydactyl (see page 68). Today, about 60 cats live in the Ernest Hemingway Museum and Home, in Key West, Florida, protected by Hemingway's will. About half of these are polydactyl and may be descendants of the original cat. Hemingway often named his cats after movie stars and characters in his books.

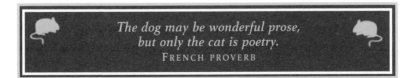

The dog may be wonderful prose,
but only the cat is poetry.
FRENCH PROVERB

MUSICAL CATS

OWNER	OCCUPATION	CAT
Aleksandr Borodin (1833–87)	Russian composer	Dlinyenki, Rybolov, Tommy
Michael Feinstein (1956–)	American singer	Bing Clawsby
Roberta Flack (1939–)	American singer	Caruso
Robert Goulet (1933–2007)	American actor and singer	Vincent and Wart
Whitney Houston (1963–2012)	American R & B singer	Marilyn Miste
Jean-Michel Jarre (1948–)	French composer/ performer	Woody and Allen
Cyndi Lauper (1953–)	American singer and actress	Weasel
John Lennon (1940–80)	ex-Beatle	Elvis
Paul McCartney (1942–)	ex-Beatle	Martha
Charles Mingus (1922–79)	American jazz bassist	Nightlife
Richard Patrick (1968–)	American rock musician	Pony Boy, Soda Pop
Henri Sauguet (1901–89)	French composer	Cody

Domenico Scarlatti's (1685–1757) cat Pulcinella inspired *The Cat's Fugue* because she liked to walk up and down his keyboards.

Frédéric Chopin (1810–49) copied some of the notes his cat played when it jumped on the keyboard while he was composing his *Cat Waltz (Valse brilliante in A minor, opus 34, #3).*

Away from the spotlight and microphone, Freddie Mercury (1946–92), the well-known vocalist for the English rock band Queen, was a dedicated cat man. While on tour, Freddie regularly telephoned home to talk to Oscar, Tiffany, Delilah, Goliath, Miko, Romeo, and Lily for hours at a time. He dedicated his first solo album, *Mr. Bad Guy,* to them and cat lovers everywhere. His favorite cat, Delilah, received the ultimate accolade when he wrote a song for her.

TOP CATS

OWNER	OCCUPATION	CAT
Tony Blair (1953–)	British prime minister	Humphrey*
George W. Bush (1946–)	U.S. president	India
Georges Clemenceau (1841–1929)	French statesman	Prudence
Bill Clinton (1946–)	U.S. president	Socks
Charles de Gaulle (1890–1970)	French president	Gris-Gris
Stephen Harper (1959–)	Canadian prime minister	Cheddar
Czar Nicholas I (1796–1855)	Russian emperor	Vashka
Joseph Stalin (1879–1953)	Leader of the Soviet Union	Samson
Queen Victoria (1819–1901)	British monarch	White Heather

*Humphrey was not the Blairs' cat, but came with the prime minster's residence.

Crown Prince Thutmose, an Egyptian prince, had his beloved cat Ta-Miu mummified and laid in an elaborately decorated sarcophagus.

In the ninth century, cat lover King Henry I (1068–1135) of Saxony in England introduced a fine of 60 bushels of corn for killing a cat.

Chu Hou-Tsung (1507–66), the 11th Emperor of the Ming Dynasty in China, had a beloved cat called Shuang-mei. She accompanied the emperor everywhere and when she died, he placed a stone tablet on her grave inscribed with the epitaph *Ch'iu-lung Chung,* meaning "The Grave of a Dragon with Two Horns," the highest tribute that could be paid to a person, let alone a cat.

Robert E. Lee (1807–70), the Confederate Army General during the American Civil War, traveled with several cats, whom he mentioned in letters home to his family. He reported being lonely, with only his dog and cats for company. Despite Spec the dog's jealousy, he allowed the cats to share his tent because they were comforting and kept the mice under control.

King Charles I of England (1600–49) had complete faith in his cat, called Cat, who was his lucky mascot. By strange coincidence, Cat died the day before the king was arrested and later beheaded.

TINSELTOWN TABBIES

OWNER	OCCUPATION	CAT
Ann-Margret (1941–)	Swedish actress	Big Red, Tuff,
Warren Beatty (1937–)	American movie actor	Cake
Jeanne Beker (1952–)	Canadian TV personality	Marcel
George Burns (1896–1996)	American comedian	Willie
Walter Cronkite (1916–2009)	American TV newsman	Dancer
Doris Day (1924–2019)	American movie actress	Punky
Phyllis Diller (1917–2012)	American comedian	Mr. Cat
Vivica A. Fox (1964–)	American actress	Sheba, Snookie, Tigger
James Franco (1978–)	American actor	Sammy, Zelda
Van Heflin (1910–71)	American movie actor	Mousetrap, Silkhat
Janet Leigh (1927–2004)	American actress	Turkey
Vivien Leigh (1913–67)	British actress	Boy, New, Nichols, Poo Jones
Marilyn Monroe (1926–62)	American actress	Mitsou
Martin Mull (1943–)	American actor	Alice
Kim Novak (1933–)	American movie actress	Pyewacket
Gary Oldman (1958–)	English movie actor	Soymilk, nicknamed Mook
Bernadette Peters (1944–)	American actress/singer	Murphy
Dedee Pfeiffer (1964–)	American actress	Billy
Regis Philbin (1931–)	American talk show host	Sara, Sascha
Stephanie Powers (1942–)	American movie actress	Señor
Sally Jessy Raphaël (1935–)	American talk show host	Sheba
Molly Ringwald (1968–)	American actress	Tigerlily
Gene Shalit (1932–)	American TV book critic	Fellini
Martha Stewart (1941–)	American TV personality	Beethoven, Mozart, Teeny, Vivaldi
Elizabeth Taylor (1932–2011)	American movie actress	Jeepers Creepers
Joan Van Ark (1943–)	American actress	Asole, Carream, El C
Robert Wagner (1930–)	American movie/TV actor	Dweezil

🐾 The actress Elizabeth Taylor gave James Dean (1931–55) a kitten called Marcus in 1955, when they were filming *Giant* together. He left Marcus with a girlfriend the night before the day he was killed while driving his car in 1955.

🐾 Patrick Stewart adopted his beloved cat, whom he called Bella, on the set of *Star Trek: The Next Generation* (1987).

OTHER FAMOUS CAT OWNERS

🐾 Sizi was the feline friend of Nobel Peace Prize-winning French missionary and surgeon, Albert Schweitzer. Although left-handed, when Sizi fell asleep on his left arm, Schweitzer wrote prescriptions with his right hand so he wouldn't disturb her.

🐾 Egyptian-born Jean-Claude Suarès (1942–2013), a New York illustrator, was not allowed to own a cat or a car when he lived in Egypt. However, once he moved to the United States he became the proud owner of a Rolls Royce—and a cat.

🐾 The electrical engineering wizard, Nikola Tesla (1856–1943), developer of the spark plug, said that his curiosity about electrical things was first stirred while he was stroking his pet cat Macak. One particularly cold, dry evening, as he was running his hand down Macak's back, he was amazed to see the cat's fur glow with light and generate sparks. Later, as Macak tiptoed across the room, he shook his paws as if he were walking over wet grass and an incredulous Tesla noticed the cat's body was surrounded by a distinct aura of light, like a halo. His desire to understand and explain what was going on led Tesla to make great advances in electric lighting, radio, radar, remote control, and early computers.

🐾 Florence Nightingale, the Lady with the Lamp who famously nursed the British troops wounded in the Crimean War, lived with Disraeli, Gladstone, and Bismarck—because she always named her Persian cats after important men.

CHAPTER 3

Fictional Cats

The multifaceted cat has been rich grist to the creative mill since the dawn of civilization. The elegant, graceful, and mysterious cat has been an inspiration to painters and sculptors, poets and story-tellers—conveying menace, dispensing wisdom, solving crimes, and abetting witches aplenty. Cartoonists have brilliantly exploited the smart, fastidious, disdainful cat, stripping away its dignity and superiority by turning the tables on it in those legendary rivalries between cats and mice and cats and dogs, with hilarious results.

POETIC PUSSYCATS

The first authoritative book on cats was written by François-Augustin Paradis de Moncrif (1687–1770). While there's always been plenty to say about cats, no one has written a longer poem about them than the Spanish author Lope Felix de Vega-Carpio (1562–1635), who wrote the epic poem *La Gatomaquia*, or the *Battle of the Cats*. It tells the story of two tomcats, Marramaquiz and Micifuz, who bicker and fight to win the heart of a female cat, Zapaquilda—for 2,500 verses.

Charles Dickens (1812–70) may have loved cats but, in his novel *Bleak House*, he made Lady Jane, Mr. Krook's large gray cat, vicious and sinister with "tigerish" claws. Just like the law, the main target of the book, once she had trapped something in her claws, she would never let it go.

The Cat in the Hat (1958) is a children's early reading book about an anarchic cat in a hat, written in rhyme by Dr. Seuss (1904–91). One rainy day the Cat in the Hat appears at a house to amuse two children while their mother is away. He brings with him two creatures, Thing One and Thing Two, and does crazy tricks to amuse the children, despite the objections of a responsible goldfish. Although his zany antics create chaos, he cleans up the mess before the mother returns.

PUSS IN BOOTS

Puss in Boots, the story of a clever cat who plays various tricks to help his poor master become rich, is best known from the version written by the French author Charles Perrault (1628–1703) in 1697, but there are earlier versions. This popular European folktale has been made into ten movies and an opera, and the character turned up in the 2004 DreamWorks movie *Shrek 2*—its voice was supplied by Antonio Banderas.

Cats from *Old Possum's Book of Practical Cats* by T. S. Eliot, in alphabetical order:

Admetus
Alonzo
Augustus
Bill Bailey
Bombalurina
Bustopher Jones
Cat Morgan
Coricopat
Demeter
Electra
George
Gilbert
Great Rumpus Cat, The
Griddlebone
Growltiger
Grumbuskin
Gus (aka Asparagus)
James

Jellylorum
Jennyanydots
Jonathan
Macavity
Mr. Mistoffelees
Mungojerrie
Munkustrap
Old Deuteronomy
Oopsa Cat (aka James Buz-James)
Peter
Plato
Quaxo
Rum Tum Tugger, The
Rumpelteazer (*Note:* Spelled "Rumpleteazer" in the musical)
Skimbleshanks, The Railway Cat
Tumblebrutus
Victor

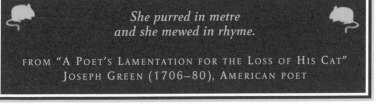

*She purred in metre
and she mewed in rhyme.*

FROM "A POET'S LAMENTATION FOR THE LOSS OF HIS CAT"
JOSEPH GREEN (1706–80), AMERICAN POET

BEATRIX POTTER'S CATS

CAT	TALE
White cat watching the goldfish in Mr. McGregor's pond	*The Tale of Peter Rabbit* (1902)
Simpkin	*The Tailor of Gloucester* (1902)
Tabby cat, who sits on the basket under which Peter Rabbit and Benjamin Bunny are hiding	*The Tale of Benjamin Bunny* (1904)
Tabby Kitten washing her white paws when Lucie meets her	*The Tale of Mrs. Tiggy-Winkle* (1905)
Mrs. Ribby, cousin of Tabitha Twitchit	*The Tale of the Pie and the Patty-Pan* (1905) *The Roly-Poly Pudding* (1908)
Moppet	*The Story of Miss Moppet* (1906)
Tom Kitten Moppet and Mittens	*The Tale of Tom Kitten* (1907) *The Roly-Poly Pudding* (1908)
Mrs. Tabitha Twitchit	*The Tale of Tom Kitten* (1907) *The Tale of the Pie and the Patty-Pan* (1905)
Ginger	*The Tale of Ginger and Pickles* (1909)
Ginger cat	*The Tale of Johnny Town-Mouse* (1918)
Susan, a white cat Large yellow ship's cat	*The Tale of Little Pig Robinson* (1930)

Note: The Roly-Poly Pudding was republished as *The Tale of Samuel Whiskers* in 1928.

ORLANDO

Many generations of young children have been captivated by the adventures of *Orlando, the Marmalade Cat,* created by Kathleen Hale (1898–2000) in 1938. Each story is illustrated by her bright, colorful drawings of Orlando, the plump orange tabby cat with green eyes, living his happy life with Grace, his tabby wife, and their kittens, Pansy, Mabel, and Tinkle.

FELINES IN FANTASY

In *Harry Potter and the Prisoner of Azkaban,* while in her third year at Hogwarts, Hermione Granger acquires a pet cat/kneazle-cross named Crookshanks. (A kneazle is a catlike creature with large ears, spotted fur, and a lionlike tail that is seriously more intelligent than a cat.) From the beginning, the intuitive Crookshanks had been suspicious of Ron Weasley's pet rat, Scabbers, whom he eventually unmasks as Peter Pettigrew. He had been a friend of Harry's parents James and Lily, until he revealed their whereabouts to the wicked Voldemort on the night of their murders.

Fans of Terry Pratchett's *Discworld* series of books will recognize Greebo as the scarred, cantankerous, vampire-eating British Blue cat with one eye belonging to Nanny Ogg, who makes his first appearance in *Wyrd Sisters.* Greebo's nemesis is You, a little white kitten owned by the witch, Granny Weatherwax, who had scratched Greebo's face so severely that he stayed away from her afterward.

Another cat appears in a Terry Prachett novel—Maurice is the star of *The Amazing Maurice and his Educated Rodents* (2001).

In Terry Brooks' fantasy series set in the *Magic Kingdom of Landover* (1986), Edgewood Dirk is a Prism Cat, with gleaming emerald eyes and a silver-gray coat with black paws, face, and tail. Prism cats are old and rare. Edgewood Dirk is one of the few survivors, if not the only remaining member of an old race of fairy creatures. He can capture light from any source and transform it into energy—to create a fire or to battle a witch.

IN THE MOVIES

FILM	CAT	ROLE
Adventures of Milo and Otis (1989)	Milo	As a kitten, Milo befriends Otis, a puppy, and they have adventures together.
Austin Powers: International Man of Mystery (1997)	Mr. Bigglesworth	Dr. Evil's cat, a parody of Blofeld's cat in the Bond movies.
Babe (1995)	Duchess	The spiteful cat who tells the young pig Babe that all pigs eventually get eaten.
Bedknobs and Broomsticks (1971)	Cosmic Creepers	Miss Eglantine Price, a witch and Charlie's nanny, owns Cosmic Creepers, a scary cat that chases Charlie when he's turned into a white rabbit.
Cat's Eye (1985)	General	Saves a little girl from being suffocated by a troll.
Catwoman (2004)	Midnight	Played by several Egyptian Mau cats, Midnight breathes life into Patience Philips (played by Halle Berry), turning her into Catwoman.
The Three Lives of Thomasina (1964)	Thomasina	A strained relationship between father and daughter is healed when a "dead" cat magically reappears.

COMIC STRIP CATS

Heathcliff, a rebellious ginger cat who is always getting into trouble, first appeared in a comic strip in 1973. Over the years he has costarred with a large dog called Marmaduke, and then with the Catillac Cats, a gang of alley cats led by Riff Raff and featuring smart guy Wordsworth, silly Mungo, and wimpish Hector, all up against bad dog Leroy. He lives with Grandpa, Grandma, Iggy, and Marcy Nutmeg and has a gorgeous white Persian girlfriend.

Garfield is a lazy, selfish, overweight, orange tabby cat who enjoys eating, sleeping, stealing his owner's dinner, and tormenting Odie by kicking him off the table. He loves lasagna and enjoys entertaining (or annoying) an unseen neighborhood audience on top of a fence in the middle of the night (and gets bombarded by various objects by the agitated audience for it). He hates spiders, and often splats them with a rolled up newspaper. His first comic-strip appearance was on June 19, 1978. His first television appearance was on *Here Comes Garfield,* and his last was on the *Garfield and Friends* episode, *The Ocean Blue.* James Garfield Davis, who is the grandfather of Jim Davis, the creator of the Garfield comic strip, was named after President James A. Garfield. In turn, Jim Davis named the character Garfield after his grandfather. Other Garfield cat characters include:

- Arlene, a pink siren of a cat, is Garfield's girlfriend
- Garfield's nephew Normal professes to be the world's cutest kitten
- Sonja is Garfield's mother
- Penelope, another love interest for Garfield, lives in an Italian restaurant.

In the comic strip Dilbert, created by Scott Adams, Catbert first appeared in 1994 as the "evil Director of Human Resources," where he spends much of his time coming up with ways to torment the employees. The comic strip brings to light the unpleasant white-collar work conditions that can occur in the corporate world.

Cartoonist Berkeley Breathed first developed the character Bill the Cat for his comic strip Bloom County in the 1980s. He has also featured in Outland and Opus and has appeared in the children's book *A Wish for Wings That Work,* which has been made into an animated television special.

ANIMATED CATS

The first animated cat was Krazy Kat, a cartoon strip drawn by George Herriman that made the transition from paper to film in 1916.

Gay Purr-ee, released in 1962, is a full-length movie with feline starring roles. Judy Garland was the voice of the star Mewsette, one of the last parts she played.

In his early days, Disney's Mickey Mouse outsmarted a rough cat called Pete. As years went on, Pete eventually fell by the wayside, thus leaving Disney with no cat at all in their core group of characters.

Tom and Jerry first appeared together in 1939 in *Puss Gets the Boot*. The dueling feline-rodent partnership, created by Fred Quimby, William Hanna, and Joseph Barbera, won seven Oscars in 18 years.

Sylvester J. Pussycat, Sr. is a three-time Academy Award-winning cat that appeared in more than 90 Looney Tunes and Merrie Melodies animated cartoons made from 1945 to 1965. Sylvester's pet hate is Tweety Pie, a tiny baby-faced canary in a cage, who is always getting the better of the unlucky cat. Sylvester's trademark expletive is "Thufferin' Thuccotash," delivered in a sloppy lisp. Tweety Pie is noted for saying "I tawt I taw a puddy tat."

Hanna-Barbera launched Top Cat on ABC on September 27, 1961. T. C. to his friends, Top Cat was a fast-talking, wheeler-dealer alley cat that lived with his gang, Choo Cho, Fancy-Fancy, Spook, The Brain, and Benny the Ball, in Hoagy's Alley in New York City.

Courageous Cat and his sidekick Minute Mouse, a crime-fighting duo, live in the Cat Cave, drive around in the Catmobile, and carry Catguns. The cartoon first appeared in 1960 and was invented by Bob Crane as a parody of his earlier hit, *Batman*.

THE SIMPSONS

The Simpsons haven't had a lot of luck with their cats, all of whom they called Snowball, regardless of color or season. In fact, three Snowballs died in a single episode, *I D'oh-Bot*.

First there was Snowball, a sometimes white, sometimes black female cat. Snowball was never actually seen in the series except in flashback; however, she was mentioned several times. Sadly, she was run over and killed by a drunken Clovis Quimby, the mayor's brother. From various references, there seems to be some confusion about exactly when she died, but probably around Halloween 1990. Although her television appearances are rare, there are many "touching" dedications to Snowball in the Simpsons literature.

Young Lisa Simpson was inconsolable when her beloved Snowball died. Homer and Marge tried to fool her by replacing the deceased cat with an identical one, but Snowball II never healed the aching hole in Lisa's heart. Snowball II appeared in the episode *Simpsons Roasting on an Open Fire*. Poor old Snowball II went to kitty heaven after being hit by Dr. Hibbert's Mercedes Benz G500 in the episode of *I D'oh-Bot*.

Lisa chose Snowball III, an orange cat, from an animal shelter shortly after Snowball II's demise. However, he died almost as soon as they got home, when he drowned trying to catch a goldfish in an aquarium.

It was straight back to the animal shelter, where a reluctant Lisa picked out a little white kitten, called Coltrane, who reminded her of Bart. On arriving home, Lisa put on some music, which scared the now renamed Snowball IV so much that he jumped out of the window and fell to his death.

Snowball V (also known as Snowball II, so it could use the old Snowball II's food bowl to save money), was the next one to arrive on the scene. Lisa advises the black cat to scram because she has bad luck with cats, but changes her mind when Snowball V misses being run over by Gil Gunderson.

ARTISTS' INSPIRATION

A close look at Albrecht Dürer's (1471–1528) engraving of *Adam and Eve* (1504)—not to be confused with the oil painting by the artist that has the same name—reveals a cat resting at the feet of the sinful couple in the Garden of Eden. Given the time in which Dürer was working, when symbolism was important in works of art, it is likely that the cat depicts evil. However, apparently all innocence has not yet been lost, because the cat is ignoring a mouse that is barely a whisker's length away from the end of its nose.

At first sight, Francisco Goya's (1746–1828) portrait of a young Spanish aristocrat *Don Manuel Osorio de Zuñiga* (1787) seems to be a sweet picture of a small boy surrounded by his pets. However, a closer look reveals that two cats are eyeing up the magpie, which is tethered to a string the little boy is holding. With this fairly blatant symbolism, Goya is expressing his disdain for the power of the aristocracy.

In Édouard Manet's (1832–83) sensational portrait of *Olympia* (1863), it's easy to be distracted by the naked prostitute reclining on her pillows and miss the little black kitten at the end of the bed. Cat and Kitten can be seen at Musée d'Orsay, Paris, France.

From his sketches of Peter, his black-and-white kitten, Louis Wain (1860–1939) created a whole world of colorful large-eyed anthropomorphized cats and kittens, wearing snazzy clothes and having a good time, playing cards or musical instruments, smoking, fishing, or simply partying. His often satirical paintings were popular in his day and widely used to illustrate children's books, greetings cards, and postcards.

One of Pierre Auguste Renoir's (1841–1919) favorite subjects was a young girl with a snoozing cat snuggled on her lap. *Sleeping Girl with a Cat* (1880) resides in the Sterling & Francine Clark Institute, Williamstown, Massachusetts; *Mademoiselle Julie Manet with Cat* (1867) hangs in Musée d'Orsay, Paris, France.

🐾 Paul Gauguin (1848–1903) could not resist adding a sleeping cat to the painting he entitled *Eiaha Ohipa* (1896), which means "Doing Nothing" in Tahitian. Now the young couple and their cat do nothing but hang in the Pushkin Museum of Fine Art, Moscow, Russia.

🐾 John Sloan's (1871–1951) portrayal of two children building a snowman in a snowy backyard in *Backyards, Greenwich Village* (1914) contains two lean cats: one hunched up against the cold on a fence, another unable to resist creeping through the snow to see what the children are doing. This snapshot of one winter's day in Greenwich Village now resides in the Whitney Museum, New York City.

🐾 In 1939, during the bitter conflict of the Spanish Civil War, Pablo Picasso (1881–1973) painted his *Cat and Bird*, showing a cat with sharp claws and a struggling wounded bird in its mouth, as a commentary on the cruel regime of General Franco's government.

🐾 Soon after moving to Paris in 1910, Marc Chagall (1887–1985) painted *Paris Through the Window* (1913), with a cat sitting on a windowsill, calmly watching the vibrant city beyond the tranquility of the room. This cat's-eye view of Paris now hangs in the Solomon R. Guggenheim Museum in New York City.

🐾 When the American printmaker Max Kahn (1903–2005) showed a cat walking elegantly in his lithograph *Cat Walk,* he failed to notice that cats move both legs on one side of the body forward at the same time—his cat has its front left leg and rear right leg forward together.

🐾 A simple but beautiful Egyptian bronze of a mother cat and her kittens has been found. It is over 2,500 years old but could have been cast yesterday.

CHAPTER 4

Cat Myths, Folklore, and Legends

Today, with the cat's popularity on the rise, it seems as though cats can't put a paw wrong, but that wasn't always the case. In days gone by, their amazing hunting skills, nocturnal habits, and mysterious behavior provoked strong human reactions, ranging from adulation to ruthless persecution. In less enlightened times, the seemingly magical powers of the cat were seen as a threat to the authorities, and many fanciful legends, folklore, and superstitions were devised to account for the seemingly inexplicable.

LIFE AMONG THE EGYPTIANS

The myth of a cat having nine lives probably originated in ancient Egypt. The priests in On, now a suburb of Cairo, worshipped Atum-Ra, a sun god who gave life to the gods of air, moisture, earth, and sky, who, in turn, produced Osiris, Isis, Seth, and Nephthys. This family of gods is known as the Ennead, or the Nine. Atum-Ra, who adopted the form of a cat to visit the underworld, embodied nine lives in one creator.

In ancient Egypt, it was believed that cats captured the life-giving rays of the setting sun in their eyes to keep them safe until morning.

Cats were believed to have powers that influenced marriage, health, children, and prosperity. The domestic goddess, Bast or Bastet, depicted as a sitting or standing cat-headed woman, became Egypt's most popular deity. Bast was often shown holding an utchat, the sacred eye with magical powers. An utchat with a cat and her kittens inside the eye was given as a wedding present to bless the couple with children.

If a cat died, an ancient Egyptian mourned by shaving off his eyebrows and mummifying the cat; embalmed mice were placed in its tomb.

> *O sacred cat! Your mouth is the mouth of the god Atum, the lord of life who has saved you from all taint.*
>
> A 4TH-CENTURY B.C. SONG OF PRAISE FROM EGYPT

ALL ROADS LEAD TO ROME

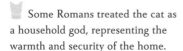

Some Romans treated the cat as a household god, representing the warmth and security of the home.

Cats were the only animal allowed in Roman temples.

At Roman weddings, sacrifices were made to the cat to bless the couple with a prosperous future.

Sacrifices were also made to the cat at Roman funerals, thereby ensuring protection for the deceased in the afterlife.

One Roman myth tells how Diana, the great hunter and goddess of the moon, was transformed into a cat to escape from Typhon, a monstrous hundred-headed dragon.

The ancient Romans appreciated cats, but perhaps not as much as the Egyptians. Legend has it that the tension between the two countries began with the death of a cat. When Caesar occupied the banks of the River Nile in 47 B.C., a Roman was stoned by the people of Alexandria

after he killed a cat. From then onward, cats were outlawed in Roman-occupied Egypt.

As a free spirit, the cat is most closely associated with the goddess of liberty and freedom, Libertas, in Roman mythology. Roman statues of the goddess were often depicted with a cat at her feet. The Roman author Pliny the Elder wrote in his book *Naturalis Historia* (Natural Stories) that the Roman world appreciated cats for their independent nature.

CAT PROVERBS

Cats have inspired much wisdom and homespun philosophy. The accumulated wisdom expressed so succinctly in these proverbs, which come from all ages and around the world, pays handsome tribute to the fascinating nature and behavior of cats.

PROVERB	COUNTRY OF ORIGIN
An old cat will not learn how to dance.	Morocco
After dark, all cats are leopards.	Native North American
He who plays with a cat must bear its scratches.	Yiddish
The widow gave orders to her cat and the cat gave them to its tail.	China
The cat dreams of garbage.	Hindu
A cat is a lion in a jungle of small bushes.	India
A mother-in-law and a daughter-in-law in one house are like two cats in a bag.	Yiddish
A cat has nine lives. For three he plays, for three he strays, and for the last three he stays.	England
A cat with a straw tail keeps away from fire.	England
A house without either a cat or a dog is the house of a scoundrel.	Portugal
Beware of people who dislike cats.	Ireland
Books and cats and fair-haired little girls make the best furnishings for a room.	France
Cats don't catch mice to please God.	Afghanistan
Happy owner, happy cat. Indifferent owner, reclusive cat.	China

PROVERB	COUNTRY OF ORIGIN
A cat will teach her young ones all the tricks, except how to jump backward.	Dutch Antilles
If stretching were wealth, the cat would be rich.	Africa
In a cat's eyes, all things belong to cats.	England
One should not send a cat to deliver cream.	Yiddish
Handsome cats and fat dung heaps are the sign of a good farmer.	France
Curiosity killed the cat, satisfaction brought it back.	England
The cat's a saint when there are no mice about.	Japan
To live long, eat like a cat, drink like a dog.	German
When the mouse laughs at the cat, there's a hole nearby.	Nigeria
Wherever the mice laugh at the cat, there you will find a hole.	Portugal
Who cares well for cats will marry as happily as he or she could ever wish.	French
The cat is nature's beauty.	France
You will always be lucky if you know how to make friends with strange cats.	North America
You come with a cat and call it a rabbit.	Cameroon
The dog for the man, the cat for the woman.	England
It takes a good many mice to kill a cat.	Unknown
A cat may go to a monastery, but she still remains a cat.	Ethiopia
Honest as the cat when the meat is out of her reach.	England

CHRISTIAN, JEWISH &
ISLAMIC CAT LORE

Ancient Hebrew folklore tells how the first cats were created on the Ark. Apparently, before the flood there were no cats, but a pair of lions had gone onboard. During the voyage, the Ark was overrun with mice, eating the ship's stores. Noah prayed for a solution. God proposed that Noah should whack the sleeping male lion on the nose. When he did, the lion sneezed, and out of his nostrils popped the first pair of cats.

A postscript to this story says that God created cats but the mouse was the Devil's handiwork. Mice set out to destroy all life on the earth by gnawing holes in the Ark, but God's cats saved the day—and frogs plugged the holes.

During their cat-hating days, Christians blamed the Devil for creating cats by accident when he was actually trying to put a human being together. At first, the poor cat was bald, until a compassionate St. Peter gave it a warm fur coat.

Various cultures have different ways of explaining how tabby cats came by the distinctive M marking on their foreheads. According to Christian legend, a little cat gained favor with Mary, the mother of Jesus, in the stable in Bethlehem where Jesus was born, by cuddling up beside the crying baby to keep him warm and soothe him with its purring. The grateful Mary awarded the cat the special sign of her initial on its forehead, which it has worn ever since.

In the Islamic tradition, the prophet Mohammed is known to have loved cats because one saved his life when a snake crawled up his sleeve. The wily cat called upon to remove the snake asked it to poke its head out so the terms of its departure could be discussed. As soon as the snake's head appeared at the edge of the sleeve, the cat grabbed it and carried it away. As its reward, the cat was given the symbol of a dark M on its forehead to remind everybody how much it had pleased Mohammed. By and large, cats are still treated well in the Islamic world—unlike dogs, they're even allowed inside mosques.

CAT PHRASES

WORDS AND PHRASES	MEANING	ORIGINS
No room to swing a cat	Suggests that space in a house or room is cramped.	*Cat* was shortened from *cat-o'-nine-tails*, a whip used to punish sailors; space in old ships was restricted; a whip couldn't be used belowdecks. Alternatively, swinging a cat around by its tail used to be a popular but cruel sport.
Sick as a cat	Very sick.	Many cats vomit up fur balls on a regular basis.
It's raining cats and dogs	Referring to a heavy downpour in a storm.	In ancient European mythology, cats were believed to control the weather, dogs the winds. A storm was seen as their combined efforts. Also, in England, cats and dogs liked to sleep on a warm thatched roof. When it rained heavily, the straw or reeds got slippery and the cats and dogs slid off into the street below.
Like a cat on hot bricks/Like a cat on a hot tin roof	A jumpy person who wants to get out of an uncomfortable spot.	Presumably from observing cats skip over hot surfaces, unable to settle.
When the cat's away, the mice will play	To take advantage of the absence of a person in authority.	Mice and rats soon proliferate when there is no cat around to keep their numbers down.
To let the cat out of the bag	To reveal a secret.	Possibly refers to when farmers carried piglets to market in a sack. Some farmers put a cat into the sack instead of a pig to sell, sight unseen, to an unwary farmer.

WORDS AND PHRASES	MEANING	ORIGINS
Before the cat can lick her ears	Something that will never happen.	No matter how much a cat twists, it can never lick its ears.
A cat in gloves catches no mice	You can't always get what you want by being polite and gentle.	Cats obviously need to extend their claws to catch mice.
Put the cat among the pigeons	To stir up trouble, often by deliberately revealing a secret.	When Great Britain ruled India, one sport was to put a cat in a cage with pigeons and bet on how many birds the cat could catch in a single swipe.
Cat got your tongue?	Why aren't you saying anything?	Probably dates to the old Middle Eastern practice of cutting out a liar's tongue and feeding it to the king's cats.
There's more than one way to skin a cat	There are various ways of tackling a task.	This refers to the many ways of skinning a catfish, not a cat.
As weak as a kitten	As helpless and feeble as a newborn kitten.	Kittens are blind and deaf at birth and totally depend on their mother's care.
Cat-in-hell's chance (derived from *"No more chance than a cat in hell without claws"*)	No prospect of success.	Meaning that you have to go into a fight properly armed to stand any chance of winning.
Cat calls	To heckle a bad stage performance with whistles and boos.	Dates back to Shakespearean times, when audiences often expressed their dissatisfaction and impatience by jeering the actors with catlike sounds.
Catnap	A short snooze.	Alluding to the cat's ability to fall asleep anywhere, at any time, for as long or as briefly as possible.

WORDS AND PHRASES	MEANING	ORIGINS
Catwalk	A narrow, often raised walkway, used in fashion shows.	A tribute to the cat's ability to walk along very narrow places without losing its balance.
Copycat	A person who copies somebody else.	Refers to the way kittens learn by copying their mother.
Fight like cats and dogs	People who argue fiercely without any sign of resolution.	Self-explanatory cat vs. dog situation.
Cat's whiskers; Cat's meow	Referring to something that is excellent.	Thomas A. Dorgan (1877–1929), an American cartoonist, is credited with popularizing both expressions.
Curiosity killed the cat	A warning to be careful when investigating the unknown.	This was originally "Care kills a cat."
Having kittens	When a person is hysterical, panicking, or absolutely furious.	In medieval times, it was thought that a painful pregnancy meant that the mother was cursed by a witch, so was carrying kittens, which were scratching inside her. This made the mother-to-be panic.
Grinning like a Cheshire cat	An inane grin that is hard to remove.	From *Alice's Adventures in Wonderland* by Lewis Carroll.

Try curiosity.

DOROTHY PARKER (1893–1967), AMERICAN WIT AND WRITER, WHEN ASKED HOW TO KILL A CAT

WORDS AND PHRASES	MEANING	ORIGINS
Look like a cat that swallowed a canary	Someone with a self-satisfied grin.	Just like a cat might have if it had eaten a bird it had caught.
Look what the cat dragged in	A wry comment when someone unwelcome turns up.	Reflects the way that cats bring home their catches looking the worse for wear.
Playing cat and mouse	Playing a strategic game or playing in a cruel or taunting way.	Like a cat toying with a mouse.
Pussyfooting about	Show reluctance to commit or to proceed warily without resolve.	Alluding to a hunting cat's great stealth, followed by its delay in finishing off its victim.
Scaredy cat	A taunt at someone who reneges on a dare or is timid.	Reflects the cat's fear of confronting a large dog.
See which way the cat jumps	To wait and see what's going to happen.	Dates back to putting a cat in a tree as a target; the gunman waited to see which way the cat would move before shooting it.
Rubbing someone up the wrong way	To annoy or upset somebody.	Picking up on how much cats dislike having their fur stroked against how it naturally lies.
To get one's back up	To anger quickly.	Like a cat who arches its back and fluffs up the fur along its back when it sees a dog.
Cat burglar	Describes a nimble, stealthy, silent thief.	Like a cat that can creep up on its prey, unseen and unheard.
Sourpuss	Usually applied to a short-tempered killjoy.	Stems from when "buss" meant face or mouth, before it became "puss" for a cat.
Let sleeping cats lie	Leave things well alone.	A proverbial French version of "Let sleeping dogs lie."

DREAMING OF CATS

I f you dream of a (an) . . .

tortoiseshell cat, you will be lucky in love.

orange cat, you will be lucky in money and business.

black cat, you will be lucky.

black-and-white cat, you will have luck with children.

black-and-white cat, a child may be born.

tabby, your home and everyone who lives there will be blessed with good luck.

multicolored cat, you will have luck making friends.

white cat, you will have good luck.

two cats fighting, you will be ill or have a quarrel.

black cat, you have some doubts about using your intuition.

gray cat, you should be guided by your dreams.

cat with no tail, you may be losing your independence.

aggressive cat, you're probably having problems with your more feminine side.

I f you dream of . . .

being severely scratched by a cat, you can expect sickness and trouble.

noisy alley cats, you should avoid an indiscreet acquaintance.

seeing a cat and snake cosying up to each other, you may soon become embroiled in an angry struggle.

CHINESE BELIEFS

🐾 In Chinese legend, cats were put in charge of the world and once possessed the power of speech. However, the cats soon delegated their role to humans so that they could concentrate on relaxing. That is why cats can no longer speak and why they wear arrogant expressions when they see people dashing about.

🐾 Another Chinese myth relates how cats are supernatural creatures that can detect ghosts. The cat god, Li Shou, is said to afford protection against the evil spirits of the night.

🐾 According to one legend, the Jade Emperor, ruler of Heaven and Earth, invited all the beasts of the earth to appear before him in Heaven, so that he could choose just 12 of them to take their places in the Chinese zodiac. He asked the rat to organize the visit. At the time, the rat and the cat were best buddies, so the cat, who was afraid of oversleeping, asked his friend to wake him when they were ready to leave for Heaven. However, the rat was worried that he wouldn't be selected because he was ugly compared with his handsome

friend, so he didn't wake him. When the cat found out that he'd missed his chance to be part of the zodiac because of the rat's treachery, he was furious and swore to be the rat's worst enemy forever.

🐾 Another popular explanation why the cat is not in the Chinese Zodiac tells how the Jade Emperor decreed that the animals to be part of the Chinese zodiac would be decided by a race over a swift-flowing river. The cat and the rat knew that they were the worst swimmers among all the animals, but they were smart enough to work out that the best way to win would be to jump on the back of an ox, and the naive beast of burden did not protest. However, the rat wanted to win so much that he pushed his friend the cat into the water. When the ox reached the riverbank, the rat jumped off ahead of him and was awarded first place in the race for his ingenuity. The cat has never forgiven the rat—and still hates water.

🐾 Although the cat is not among the 12 animals of the Chinese Zodiac, it is in the Vietnamese Zodiac—in place of the rabbit.

JAPANESE LORE

🐾 In Japanese mythology, orange cats instead of black ones were thought to bring bad luck. The Golden Flowers (*kinkwa-neko*)—as they were called—were believed to be able to transform themselves into beautiful young women, who were capable of seducing vulnerable men. This made the Golden Flowers very powerful and threatening indeed.

🐾 The Beckoning Cat (*maneki-neko*), with one paw raised in welcome, is widely held to be a lucky mascot in Japan. According to legend, the monks living at the temple of Gotoku-ji, in what is now a suburb of Tokyo, were very poor, but they shared what little they had with a cat. One day, a group of noblemen was passing when it started to rain heavily and they were beckoned to shelter inside by the cat raising its paw. Shortly afterward, the spot where the travelers had been standing was hit by lightning. The noblemen were so grateful to the cat for saving their lives that they endowed the temple with money and restored its fortunes. Ever since, statuettes of a cat with a paw raised have been worn or displayed outside buildings as good luck charms. A cat with a raised left paw brings wealth, while one with its right paw raised brings happiness.

🐾 In Japanese folklore, a cat born with an unusual black mark on its back is said to be a spirit-bearing cat. If the mark looks like a lady in a kimono, then the cat is thought to carry the spirit of one of the owner's ancestors. Such a cat had to be carefully protected, so kimono cats were often sent to a temple for their own safety.

🐾 In Japan, religious ceremonies were held for the souls of departed cats. A Japanese myth says that cats turn into super spirits when they die.

OTHER BELIEFS FROM AROUND THE WORLD

According to Buddhism, the body of the cat is the temporary resting place of the reincarnated soul of very spiritual people who have reached their last stage on the way to heaven.

In Burma and Siam, people believed that the souls of the departed lived in the bodies of cats before moving on to the next life.

One Thai legend explains that the dark patches on the shoulders of some Siamese cats are temple marks left where the Buddha's fingers touched them in blessing.

Another legend tells of cats that saved a Thai temple's treasured golden goblet, which belonged to the Buddha, from Burmese invaders by hooking their tails around it and refusing to let go. This is said to account for the kink at the end of the tail of almost all breeds of Thai cat.

Alternatively, the kink in the tail came about when a princess went to bathe and threaded her rings over a cat's tail for safekeeping and the cat curled the end of its tail around them so they wouldn't slip off.

Malaysians venerated the cat as a godlike creature that eased their journey in the afterlife from hell to paradise. Anyone who killed a cat was sentenced to carry and stack as many coconut tree trunks as the cat had hairs.

In Indonesia, cats are thought to control the rain. If water is poured over a cat, it will summon rain. Even today, the cloud-gray Korat cat is ceremonially sprinkled with water to bring rain for the crops.

Hindus revere all living creatures but cats are special—every faithful family is expected to house and feed one.

In Indian mythology, a white cat called Patripatan was sent by his master to pick a flower from a tree in heaven. He enjoyed life in heaven with the gods so much that he completely forgot about the time and 300 years passed before he remembered that he was supposed to go back with a flower. The gods were so delighted with him that they gave him a whole branch of a beautiful tree to give to his master. On his return he found everything as he'd left it and, from then on, the country prospered in peace.

The "catgut" used to string musical instruments, tennis rackets (old wooden framed ones), and archery bows didn't normally come from cats but from the intestines of sheep. As far back as the seventeenth century, famous Italian violin makers were using sheep intestines to string their instruments; however, wanting to keep their techniques a secret, they may have indicated they were using catgut. Alternatively, catgut may have simply come about by accident after a mistranslation of the German word *kitgut*, where "kit" refers to a small fiddle, not a young cat.

Hey, diddle, diddle!
The cat and the fiddle,
The cow jumped over the moon.
NURSERY RHYME BY
EDWARD LEAR (1812–88)

In Norse mythology, Freyja, the goddess of beauty, love, and fertility, was said to ride about in a sleigh pulled by two large blue-gray long-haired cats, Brygun and Trejgun. The Finnish people believed the souls of the dead were collected by a sled pulled by cats.

Latvian farmers are delighted to find black cats around their grain silos, because they believe that they are the spirit of Rungis, a god of harvests.

In Ireland, when a visitor entered a house it was customary to say "God bless all except the cat," to show contempt for the cat, whom it was believed had evil powers over life and death.

CAT SUPERSTITIONS

Cats, especially black ones, have long been linked to luck, both good and bad. Much of the world's folklore and superstition is about cats in one shape or form. With its mysterious powers, nocturnal habits, and eyes that appeared to glow in the dark—and because they often chose to live in peace and quiet with solitary old women—the cat was associated with witchcraft and black magic. The earliest recorded incident of hundreds of cats being burned alive because they were believed to be witches in disguise took place in Metz (in what is now northeast France) in A.D. 962 on Cat Wednesday, the second Wednesday in Lent.

🐾 An early European belief was that a person could become clairvoyant by growing up with a tortoiseshell cat.

🐾 The American superstition that black cats are ill omens dates back to the Salem witch trials in 1692, when the cats belonging to the poor women accused of witchcraft were often hung with them. It led to a saying at the time, "the luck of the cat," implying bad luck, which got superimposed on the old British black-cat superstition and changed the good luck to bad.

🐾 In the Ozark Mountains of Tennessee and Arkansas, if a girl was uncertain about which answer she should give to a proposal of marriage, she would pluck three hairs from a cat's tail, put them in a folded sheet of paper, and place it under her doormat. She gave her answer according to whether the hairs formed an N or a Y when she opened the paper again.

🐾 Early American colonists believed that a broth made from boiling a black cat could cure tuberculosis—however, most were reluctant to risk the bad luck that was predicted would befall them if they killed the cat.

🐾 According to fishermen's wives, keeping a black cat at home meant that their husbands would return safely from their latest sea voyage.

Japanese sailors would often carry tortoiseshell cats (*mi-ki*) onboard ship with them to bring good luck by giving an early warning of bad weather ahead. Then they would send the cat up the mast to chase away the storm devils.

GOOD LUCK	BAD LUCK	ORIGINS
	If a black cat crosses your path	United States
If a black cat crosses your path		Great Britain
If a white cat crosses your path		United Sates
	If a white cat crosses your path	Great Britain
	Seeing a white cat at night	United States
Dreaming of a white cat		United States
A black cat walking toward you	A black cat turning and walking away from you	Worldwide
Seeing a strange black cat on your porch		Scotland
	A black cat crossing your path in moonlight; this foretells death in an epidemic	Ireland
A black cat crossing your path from left to right	A black cat crossing your path from right to left	Germany
	A black cat settling on a sickbed; the patient will die	Italy
A black cat wards off evil spirits		Japan
	A black cat fortells famine	China

CHANGING YOUR LUCK

In the early sixteenth century, anyone visiting an English home would always kiss the family cat to bring good luck.

Cat's cradle, a game played with string by children, dates back to a time in Europe when people believed that a cat could enhance the fertility of a young married couple. Shortly before the wedding, a cat in a cradle would be carried into the newlyweds' home and rocked from side to side to ensure the couple soon conceived a baby. In the string game, a hammocklike cradle is created by looping string over the fingers.

The Pennsylvania Dutch placed a cat in an empty cradle of a newlywed couple. The cat was supposed to grant their wish for children.

To reverse the bad luck curse of a black cat crossing your path, first walk in a circle, then go backward across the spot where it happened, and count to 13.

One American superstition suggests that when you see a one-eyed cat, spit on your thumb, stamp it in the palm of your hand, and make a wish. The wish will come true.

Kaspar is a sleek, black, 3-foot (90-cm) tall wooden cat that spends most of its time sitting inside a display case opposite the gift store in the world-famous Savoy Hotel in London, England. Since the 1920s, his job has been to join any table of 13 diners to increase the number to 14 and circumvent any bad luck associated with the number 13. Kaspar is seated in a chair, draped with a dinner napkin, and served each course as though he were one of the guests. The story goes that in 1898, Woolf Joel, a guest at the Savoy, hosted a dinner party for 13. He scoffed at the superstition that said the first to get up from the table would be the first to die. Joel rose first and was murdered in his native South Africa shortly afterward. After that, the Savoy commissioned Kaspar to join dinner parties of 13.

BRING MISFORTUNES

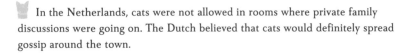

In the Netherlands, cats were not allowed in rooms where private family discussions were going on. The Dutch believed that cats would definitely spread gossip around the town.

Depending on who you were, killing a cat was supposed to bring bad luck in its aftermath because you were making a pact with the devil. For example, a farmer's cattle would die mysteriously, or you'd end up drowning if you drowned a cat. Some people took the threat of retribution so seriously they would hire professional cat hit men to do the dirty deed for them.

Scottish immigrants believed that if a cat entered a room where a dead body was lying in state, the next person to touch the cat would be blinded.

Sailors believed that throwing a cat overboard was guaranteed to bring on a storm and bring bad luck.

To meet a cat at midnight was to encounter the Devil himself.

If a cat leaves home while a person is sick and cannot be cajoled to return, that person will die.

If you wake up in the morning and see cats playing, the rest of the day will be wasted.

CHAPTER 5

Working Cats

Putting the two words "working" and "cats" side by side might seem to be a bit of an oxymoron, a contradiction in terms, given the cat's reputation for general independence, indolence, and insubordination. However, when cats are called upon to do what comes naturally to them—hunting small rodents, keeping people company, and raising morale—they excel. It has to be debatable how many are formally employed. More often than not it turns out that a cat or a kitten shrewdly adopts its workplace, then catches its keep, along with the affection of its colleagues, simply by behaving like a cat.

THE HUNTER ... AND
THE HUNTED

Writing in the fourteenth century, Geoffrey Chaucer, the most influential English poet of his day, observed that domestic cats were unreformed hunters by nature. Regardless of how well-fed and pampered they were by their owners, they had an irresistible drive to hunt and kill rodents. Not a lot has changed in the past 600 years or so since then.

> *Let's take a cat, and foster him well with milk*
> *And tender flesh, and make his couch of silk,*
> *And let him see a mouse go by the wall,*
> *Anon he waveth milk, and flesh, and all,*
> *And every dainty which is in that house,*
> *Such appetite hath he to eat a mouse.*

THE MANCIPLE'S TALE BY GEOFFREY CHAUCER (*c.* 1342–1400),
ENGLISH POET

FELINE FELON

Between 1894 and 1895, Tibbles, the feline companion to David Lyall, the lighthouse keeper on Stephen's Island, off New Zealand, achieved the dubious distinction of becoming the first and only cat to be responsible for wiping out an entire animal species. Tibbles' campaign of genocide began shortly after he arrived on the small island, when he started bringing home dead birds that Lyall didn't recognize. He sent their corpses off to the mainland for identification. By the time word came back that the bird was one of only three species of flightless songbird in the world, there were no survivors. Tibbles had probably hunted all ten breeding pairs of the ground-dwelling Stephen's Island Wren—or the Lyall wren as it's sometimes called—to extinction. Tibbles' efforts drew the following recommendation from Sir Walter Buller, a leading New Zealand ornithologist at the time:

. . . it would be as well if the Marine Department, in sending lighthouse keepers to isolated islands where interesting specimens of native birds are known or believed to exist, were to see that they are not allowed to take any cats with them, even if mousetraps have to be furnished at the cost of the state.

PEST CONTROL

It's estimated that one rat can destroy up to 1,000 pounds (455 kg) of grain every year by eating it, defecating on it, and urinating on it. Female rats have 10–12 babies per litter and can reach sexual maturity at five weeks—imagine the number of rats that would populate the world if they weren't hunted. In fact, one American author, Paul Corey (1903–92), has written in his book *Cat-Watching in the Cybernetic Age* (1977), "Eliminate cats from our ecology and, in a matter of weeks, we would be overrun by rodents."

There's plenty of ancient wisdom about how to avoid or control an infestation of mice. A Norwegian proverb states, "It's better to feed one cat than many mice." (However, a seventeenth-century proverb recommends "Keep no more cats than will catch mice.")

ANCIENT TIMES

Cats have been working for at least 4,000 years, ever since the Egyptians, who began to cultivate grain crops along the Nile Valley around 5000 B.C., realized how effective the wild cats were at controlling the mice and rats that were attacking their grain stores.

🐾 In ancient Egypt, a man and his cat, not his dog, went hunting birds together. A fragment of wall painting from the tomb of Amenemheb at Thebes in Egypt, dating from 1450 B.C., shows the dead nobleman standing up in his boat and driving birds from a reed bed with a stick. Just in front of him, his feisty feline has already caught two birds in its front and hind claws and is holding a third bird by its wings in its teeth.

🐾 The ancient Egyptians guarded their precious cats jealously—so much so that it was illegal to let cats leave Egypt. However, cats were sometimes smuggled out on Phoenician and Roman trading vessels, and they gradually colonized countries around the Mediterranean and beyond.

🐾 In recognition of the cat's vital role as rodent exterminator in guarding the nation's food supplies, the divine ruler of ancient Egypt, the pharaoh, proclaimed cats to be demigods, with all the protection afforded to divinities. To kill or injure a cat became punishable by death. In a fire, the cat had to be saved before the human occupants.

🐾 Technically, all cats in ancient Egypt were the property of the ruling pharaoh. However, for practical reasons, the cats were fostered and taken care of by the general population. The Egyptians brought their fostered cats to work at the granary overnight and picked them up again in the morning. For this important service, the foster carers received a tax credit—and they were able to claim their cats as dependents.

🐾 By 500 B.C., cats were common in China, where they were prized as protectors of precious silk cocoons.

🐾 In Buddhist temples across Asia, the cats that are kept as mousers have a pointed pattern, and may be ancestors of the Siamese breed.

🐾 When Emperor Ichijo (980–1011) of Japan decreed that cats were forbidden to work, Japan's silk industry suffered drastically. Since there were no cats around to hunt and kill the mice, the pesky critters began to destroy the silkworms and cocoons. Silk manufacturers tried positioning statues of cats around the cocoons to frighten off the mice. When this failed, the emperor bowed to common sense and ordered all cats out hunting.

🐾 In 948, Hywel Dda (Howell the Good), Prince of South Wales, passed laws to protect feline rodent hunters. The forfeit for stealing or wounding a cat was one ewe and her lamb. The penalty for killing a cat was enough grain to cover the tip of the cat's tail when the dead cat was suspended by its tail with its nose just touching the ground.

🐾 By the Middle Ages, cats were linked with witches (see page 56) and were killed. The persistent massacre of cats gave rats and their bubonic plague-carrying fleas a chance to prosper and contributed to the spread of the Black Death in Europe during the fourteenth century. Millions of people died but, ironically, in a time when survival was the main preoccupation, people stopped killing cats, whose numbers increased and helped to bring the rats under control.

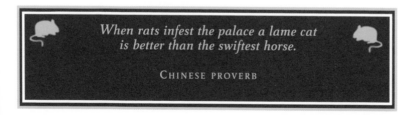

When rats infest the palace a lame cat is better than the swiftest horse.

CHINESE PROVERB

MILITARY MOUSERS

Although it's almost impossible to train or discipline cats for official military duties, they have nevertheless played small but significant roles in wars through the ages.

Cyrus II, King of the Medes and Persians, is said to have used cats to defeat an army of Egyptians in 500 B.C. Each of his soldiers was ordered to attach a live cat to his shield and hold it high to prevent the Egyptians from striking a blow. Cyrus knew that cats were sacred in Egypt and the Egyptian soldiers would not attack in case they accidentally killed a cat—which carried a penalty of death.

Centuries later, during World War II, the British forces in Burma did something similar. They painted cat images on their army vehicles and kept white cats on Army bases. When the Burmese saw this, they believed the cat's sacred spirit must favor the British, so they switched allegiance to the Allies.

On one occasion, cats were responsible for saving a ragged Egyptian army from a thumping by the much better organized Assyrian army. Apparently, overnight, before battle commenced, rats and mice got into the Assyrian stores and gnawed up the bow strings and straps on other armaments. When the Assyrians went to collect their equipment in the morning, it was useless. With cats to guard their weapons, the Egyptians still had their weapons intact.

Cats had another paw in history at the Battle of Agincourt, fought between the English and French on October 25, 1415, Saint Crispin's Day, in northern France. The story goes that the English brought their cats with them to protect their stores and their precious longbows and the French didn't. The English archers scored a famous victory that day.

In 1535, a German army used cats to spread poison gases. The troops strapped bottles of poison gas to the cats' backs, with the openings pointing toward their tails, and spooked the cats so that they panicked. As the enemy forces were lined up for battle, the frightened cats charged toward them, trailing toxic gas behind them. The enemy watched in bewilderment, then they started dropping like flies.

 During the Crimean War (1853–56), some captured Russian soldiers were found to be carrying kittens beneath their coats.

 During World War I, the British army used 500,000 cats to give their soldiers an early warning of poison gas attacks by their enemies.

 In 1942, while the Germans had the Russians pinned down in Stalingrad, a Soviet cat called Mourka risked its life trotting back and forth across a street plagued with sniper fire, carrying vital messages about enemy gun positions between Russian troops.

 In World War II, Wing Commander Guy Gibson VC was often accompanied on his missions by his cat Windy—but the cat didn't go on the famous "bouncing" bomb raid, where bombs skimmed along water to destroy German dams in 1943.

 Another airborne cat was called Salty. As a U.S. Coast Guard mascot at the San Diego Coast Guard Air Station in California, Salty managed to become the first cat to take part in a rescue mission. This happened when she stowed away, bringing her kitten with her, on an amphibian reconnaissance plane that rescued a pilot who had come down at sea.

SEAFARERS

Despite their distrust of water, cats have been going to sea in ships since time immemorial, keeping the vessel's stores rodent-free. The ship's cat was especially important in wartime, when supplies could be short, and men were far from home for extended periods and welcomed feline companionship.

SAILOR'S LUCKY CHARM

While performing their rodent extermination duties, these seafaring cats also acted as lucky mascots and mates to the crew. Sailors believed cats on ships brought good luck.

🐾 Many sailors felt that polydactyl cats—those with more toes than normal—made the best ship's cats, maybe because they could keep their balance well on a rocking vessel or were simply more successful mousers. There are more polydactyl cats found on the East Coast than in any other region of the United States, probably because sailors chose them as rat catchers to take onboard the ships that crossed from Europe to the Americas. These cats then jumped ships at the ports and bred in coastal areas.

🐾 Mascots were common on a warship during the American Civil War. The USS *Lehigh* was on blockading station in the James River, Virginia, when a photographer snapped some of the crew posing on deck with a cat.

In 1942, a kitten called Misfire was adopted as a lucky mascot at Fort Totten, New York, a fort dating back to the Civil War. The fort formed part of the United States' coastal and aerial defenses until 1967.

Simon was the ship's cat and lucky mascot on HMS *Amethyst* in 1949, during the infamous Yangtze Incident, in which the *Amethyst* was held hostage by the Chinese communist forces. When their gun batteries opened fire on the *Amethyst*, Simon was severely wounded. However, miraculously, after having four pieces of shrapnel removed, he survived, and, despite his injuries, the cat managed to visit injured shipmates, raise crew morale, and keep down a rat infestation during the incident.

One particularly lucky cat named Oscar—also known as Unsinkable Sam—served with both the German and British navies during World War II. He started out onboard the German battleship *Bismarck*. When she was sunk in 1941, the cat was seen swimming among the wreckage by a kindhearted British sailor, who took him aboard the destroyer HMS *Cossack*. However, five months later the *Cossack* went down, too—yet Oscar managed once again to live on to purr another day. He was then transferred to the aircraft carrier HMS *Ark Royal*. Unfortunately, *Ark Royal* was torpedoed by a U-boat, and Oscar was fished out of the water yet again. Having earned a reputation for being a jinx onboard ships, the cat was retired to shore-based duties, where he lived out the rest of his nine lives.

COOL CATS

Given that cats relish warm, cosy spots to curl up in, a surprising number of cats have traveled on ships to the deep-frozen wastes of Antarctica.

CAT	SHIP/EXPEDITION	FATE
NANSEN: Black-and-white kitten	Belgian sailing ship *Belgica*	Died June 22, 1897, after the ship got trapped in the ice.
BLACKWALL: Tabby and white	Robert Falcon Scott's first expedition on *Discovery* in 1901	Reached New Zealand on April 1, 1904.
POPLAR: Black cat	Robert Falcon Scott's first expedition on *Discovery* in 1901	Killed by expedition's huskies in 1904.
MORNING: Gray tabby	Sent with *Terra Nova* in 1904 to rescue *Discovery,* which had been stuck in ice	Lost overboard.
MRS. CHIPPY: Streetwise tabby tomcat	Traveled with Ernest Shackleton on *Endurance* in 1914	After being wedged in the ice for the winter, Shackleton decided to walk across the ice to the nearest land, almost 350 miles (560 km) away; Mrs. Chippy couldn't make the journey, so each member of the crew gave him a final stroke, he ate a bowl of his favorite sardines, then was terminated by a bullet.

A CAPTAIN'S LOVE

Trim was a ship's cat who loyally accompanied the explorer and navigator Captain Matthew Flinders on his voyage to map the coastline of Australia from 1801–3. Flinders' heartfelt tribute to his beloved Trim eloquently conveys how much the cat meant to him—and detailed the adventures of the cat as it traveled around the world.

To the memory of Trim,
the best and most illustrious of his Race,
the most affectionate of friends,
faithful of servants, and best of creatures.
He made the Tour of the Globe, and a voyage to Australia,
which he circumnavigated; and was ever the
delight and pleasure of his fellow voyagers.
Returning to Europe in 1803, he was shipwrecked
in the Great Equinoxial Ocean;
This danger escaped, he sought refuge and assistance
at the Isle of France, where he was made prisoner,
contrary to the laws of Justice, of Humanity,
and of French National Faith;
and where, alas! he terminated his useful career,
by an untimely death, being devoured
by the Catophagi of that island.
Many a time have I beheld his little merriments with delight,
and his superior intelligence with surprise:
Never will his like be seen again!
Trim was born in the Southern Indian Ocean, in the year 1799,
and perished as above at the Isle of France in 1804.
Peace be to his shade, and Honor to his memory.

MATTHEW FLINDERS (1774–1814),
IN MEMORY OF TRIM (1799–1804)

Trim's adventures also made him an admired cat in Australia. In 1996, a bronze statue of Trim was positioned on a window ledge of the Mitchell Library in Sydney, Australia, near a statue of his devoted captain. The Library's café is also named after the cat.

POLICE AND ENGINEERING WORK

🐾 Cats have used their rodent-catching talent to help the long arm of the law. A homeless cat, now known as Tizer, was recruited by the British Transport Police station in London's King's Cross. Since his arrival, the mouse population has suffered markedly. Tizer also enjoys a little luxury—he shares an office with a senior police officer. The Los Angeles Police Department in California has also recruited cats to control their rodent population.

🐾 The Colombian police force have been using cats to help teach rodents to detect explosives in minefields. The idea is that the rats can use their acute sense of smell to sniff out the 100,000 potentially lethal mines laid by rebels across the country. They are too light to trigger them, so the rodents were trained to freeze in front of each mine they find. However, they wouldn't stay at the spot because they feared being attacked by predators. They were shut in cages with well-fed cats, whose claws were sheathed and only played with them, which allowed the rats to get used to them and feel less anxious.

🐾 An eight-month-old stray tabby kitten from Brooklyn called Fred earned the nickname of Undercover Kitty because of the valuable work he did as a spy for the New York Police Department

> *The clever cat eats cheese and breathes down rat holes with baited breath.*
>
> W. C. FIELDS (1880–1946) AMERICAN COMEDIAN

in unmasking a bogus veterinarian operating in New York City. In February 2006, ably supported by his human sidekick, young Fred posed as a sick cat in a successful sting operation. Their suspect was later convicted of unauthorized veterinary practice, criminal mischief, injuring animals, and petty larceny.

In 1994, Snowball, a domestic cat from Prince Edward Island, Canada, helped the Mounties get their man in a murder case by participating in a pioneering piece of forensic science, which involved establishing a foolproof method for matching DNA fingerprints from samples of cat hair for the first time.

Gunnar, a gray-and-white cat, is one of 15 cats that live on the prison yard at the Kentucky State Penitentiary along Lake Barkley in western Kentucky. While the prisoners may dream of breaking out, the strays originally slithered under the perimeter fence and took up residence. The Eddyville Cats—as the prison inmates call them—have become an informal rehabilitation program at the prison. They give the prisoners something to care about and to care for. Inmates buy cat food and medical care and track down homes for the kittens among family members, prison staff, and inmates being released.

The opportunities for a cat to get involved in building one of the largest concrete structures in the world have been few and far between. However, when engineers were constructing the Grand Coulee Dam on the Columbia River in Washington in the 1930s, they had trouble threading a certain cable through a particular pipe. Some forward-thinking person proposed that a cat could solve the problem. Engineers tied a rope to the cable, tied a string to the rope, and tied the string to the cat's tail. Then the cat crawled through the pipeline and finished the job that had defeated humans—and can claim to have helped put the largest single producer of electricity in the United States in business.

IN THE DOUGH

Most millers say that the best cat to have around a flour mill is a female. Tomcats are less reliable because they will probably go off chasing the neighborhood females, and may or may not return. A female cat usually stays at home and has kittens. Having a family gives her an even greater incentive to catch more mice.

Millers preferred white cats as mousers, presumably because they were less visible against the white flour.

Mill workers would occasionally give the mill cats saucers of milk to help them deal with the toxins ingested from eating mice.

Located just north of San Francisco in the lovely wine country of Sonoma County, the Alvarado Street Bakery used to employ the services of a cat called Greta, who lived in and around the bakery and spearheaded its organic pest management program. She is now immortalized as the ginger tabby on all of the bakery's packaging.

The popular Boulangerie Patisserie au Grand Richelieu in the 1st arrondissement of Paris, dates back to 1810 and Napoleonic times, which probably makes it the city's oldest working bakery. In time-honored tradition, the bakery's cat, a gray tabby called Mimi, keeps a watchful eye and sharp claw on the raw materials used for making the daily batches of 400 baguettes, some 200 croissants, and 150 pains au chocolat.

HELP WANTED

🐾 In the San Francisco Gold Rush of 1849, miners paid approximately $50 each for the best proven rodent-hunting cats from the ship SS *Ohio*. Later, short-haired cats sold for the astronomical price of up to $100 apiece during the San Francisco rat plague of 1884.

🐾 In the 1860s, a Cairo millionaire could trace the origins of his engineering fortune back to having imported 300 cats to solve an advertised rat problem at the Suez Canal building site.

🐾 In 2004, when health officials in the state of Chihuahua in Mexico advertised for 700 cats to be sent to the isolated farming community of Atascaderos in the rugged Tarahumara mountains, they must have had high hopes of dealing with the plague of 500,000 rats that were pillaging barns and storehouses in the village. However, eight weeks later they had managed to employ the services of only 50 cats, and, with such a huge rodent population, this is one case where they had to admit that the rats had overwhelmed the cats—paws down.

🐾 Over in China in 2006, the Yangmei villagers in Sanjiang Township of Xinhui District in the city of Jiangmen, Guangdong Province, had better luck with the 200 cats they bought for 12,000 yuan ($1,500) and let loose on their problem rats. In fact, the villagers were so pleased with the hard-working cats they prepared a fish banquet for the felines to thank them for ridding their farmland of rodents.

We rat catchers might raise our fees,
Sole guardians of a nation's cheese!

FROM FABLE XXI BY JOHN GAY (1685–1732)

URBAN CATS

Just as mice and rats have adapted to city living, cats have also adjusted to urban life, where their rodent-hunting skills have remained useful to many homes and places of business.

The famous pop artist Andy Warhol (1928–87), like many other urbanites, started keeping a cat when he lived on East 75th Street, in New York City, to control the mouse population in his home. However, he developed a real passion for cats and, by the time he moved to Lexington Avenue, he had so many cats that he was giving kittens away to friends. His cats were all named Sam except for one, which was called Hester.

The city of Leeds in Yorkshire, England, has come up with a way of converting the city's feral felines from urban nuisance into valuable members of society. Feral cats are accustomed to earning their own living, and the rodent-catching skills of these semiwild cats that prefer to live outdoors are in huge demand. One pair was given to the Ilkley Golf Club in the Wharfe Valley, where they soon made themselves at home and cleared the whole golf course of rodents.

A huge tomcat called Tiger once stalked the corridors of the Ritz Hotel in London in search of rodents. On his rounds, The Terror of the Ritz found it hard to resist the tidbits of caviare and smoked salmon available. Apparently, the fat cat had to be sent to a weight-reducing course every year.

According to superstition, a cat employed to keep a theater free of rodents can bring good luck, as long as it stays backstage; if it makes a mess backstage, the performance will go even better. However, woe betide the show if it ventures on stage.

Anyone whose favorite tipple is Scotch on the rocks should be delighted to hear that the Scots guard the raw materials for making their famous whiskey jealously, with the help of cats. Indeed, the title of world's best mouser must go to Towser (1963–87), a long-haired tortoiseshell cat that worked for the Glenturret Distillery, near Crieff, on Tayside in Scotland. During her working life, the workaholic cat was reckoned to have caught, on average, three mice a day, plus sundry rats and rabbits, making a grand score of Towser 28,899–Mice 0.

> *The cat is the only animal without visible means of support who still manages to find a living in the city.*
>
> CARL VAN VECHTEN (1880–1964),
> AMERICAN WRITER AND PHOTOGRAPHER

CAT CARNIVAL

The Kattenstoet, or Cat Festival, takes place in Ypres in Belgium every third year on the second Sunday in May, harking back to a practice when the town was the center of the local wool trade. Then cats were employed to control the rodent population in the town's medieval Cloth Hall, where all the wool was stored. However, once the fleeces and cloth had been sold, the cats were no longer required and cruelly thrown down from the Hall's belfry onto the street below. Fortunately, no live cats have been tossed over the parapets since 1817. These days, the day is marked by a lively carnival, where everybody dresses up as cats to follow cat-themed floats, marching bands, jugglers, stilt walkers, and flag throwers through the town to the old Cloth Hall. There the parade culminates with velvet toy cats being cast down to the crowd below.

LIBRARY CATS

In the United States, cats are as traditional as silence in libraries, originally employed to protect the books from the nibbling teeth of rodents. There have been 697 cats recorded as official library cats around the world, with the majority in the United States. Of the 573 on record in the country, 383 have passed away after serving their institutions well, of which 22 have been immortalized as statues, and 32 are still active cats-in-residence.

JOB DESCRIPTION FOR A LIBRARY CAT

This list of the duties of a library cat is based on one drawn up by the Spencer Library of Iowa for their cat Dewey Readmore Books:

1. Reduce stress for all humans who pay attention to you.
2. Sit by the front door every morning to greet the public.
3. Sample all boxes delivered to the library for security and comfort purposes.
4. Attend all meetings as official library ambassador.
5. Provide comic relief and cuddles for librarians, readers, and borrowers whenever possible.
6. Climb in book bags and briefcases while patrons are studying or assist in retrieving any papers that fall to the floor.
7. Generate free national and worldwide publicity for your library.
8. Remember to sit still for photographs and be cute at all times.

Unlike most library cats, Maxie Speer Huett, the library cat of Maxie Speer Elementary School in Arlington, Texas, didn't live in the library, but went into work each day with the librarian, Charlie Huett, until they both retired in 2011. Although she's nearly blind, Maxie has supersonic hearing. She could detect a candy wrapper being removed from anywhere in the library and was quick to expose the culprit.

Not all library cats live among the books. The Amanda Park Timberland Library in Washington has feral library cats; Mother, Gray Papa, Grayfur, and Baby Face all dwell under the library building. The mother cats are too crafty to be caught and spayed, but they are shrewd enough to bring their kittens out to be fed by the library staff when it comes to weaning each litter. Library patrons supply food, have the kittens spayed and neutered, then adopt them.

Sometimes, an allergy to cats among the library staff or readers becomes an issue. Generally, the matter is resolved by popular vote and the cat stays on duty. Unfortunately, Muffin, the library cat for Putnam Valley, New York, wasn't so lucky. When one of the library trustees developed an allergy to cats, Muffin lost his library cat status after a long battle. However, when Muffin left, over $80,000 of private funding for the library was withdrawn by disgruntled cat lovers who want to show Muffin their support. (*Note:* Library cats usually enjoy plenty of brushing and grooming to get rid of the dander that can trigger an allergic reaction.)

Some library cats overstep their remit from time to time. In 2001, L. C., the cat-on-duty at the Escondido Public Library in California, was named in a $1.5 million claim against the City of Escondido by Richard Espinosa for "lasting physical and emotional injury." L. C. was said to have attacked Espinosa's assistance dog, which was there to protect him against panic attacks. Eventually, the claim was dismissed, but L. C. had to take early retirement and died in October 2003.

PROTECTING MUSEUMS
AND TREASURES

For the last 200 years, cats have been protecting the treasures of the magnificent State Hermitage in the heart of St. Petersburg, Russia, from the ravages of rodent interlopers. The first cats were introduced to the Winter Palace during the reign of Empress Elizabeth (1709–62), daughter of Peter the Great, who was appalled by the number of mice and rats in residence. She received five specially selected ratters from the town of Kazan in Tatarstan as a gift. Nowadays, visitors don't usually see the army of 100 or so feline security staff in the grand exhibition halls because they're hard at work catching mice and rats in the maze of corridors and stone staircases in the basement.

"It smells like cats," visitors often exclaim on visiting the Hermitage basements for the first time. To which museum staff usually reply, "Cats smell better than rats."

Originally, the czar of the day decreed that the cats should be fed and cared for by a retinue of staff paid for from the Imperial coffers. However, after the October Revolution in 1917, state funding ceased. Today, the cats take care of the Hermitage, and the museum staff take care of the cats.

Mike was the famously cantankerous feline custodian of the impressive British Museum in London, England, for almost 20 years, from February 1909 to January 1929. According to Sir Ernest A. Wallis Budge, Keeper of the Museum's Egyptian and Assyrian Antiquities, Mike always "preferred sole to whiting, and whiting to haddock, and sardines to herrings; for cod he had no use whatever. He owed much to the three gatekeepers who cooked his food for him and treated him as man and brother." However, the cat didn't always appreciate the special attention given to him. Mike would only allow Sir Ernest and the head gatekeeper to pet him, and he would always scratch any female staff who tried to stroke him.

> *He cared for none—save only two:*
> *For these he purred, for these he played,*
> *And let himself be stroked, and laid*
> *Aside his antihuman grudge—*
> *His owner—and Sir Ernest Budge!*
>
> *Old Mike, Farewell! We all regret you,*
> *Although you would not let us pet you;*
> *Of cats, the wisest oldest best cat,*
> *This be your motto—Requiescat!*
>
> ASSISTANT KEEPER HILEY, OF THE DEPARTMENT OF
> PRINTED BOOKS OF THE BRITISH MUSEUM

As a kitten, Mike got tuition from another museum cat on how to stalk pigeons. Little Mike was set to guard one flank while the house cat slowly maneuvered the pigeons up into a corner. Then each cat seized a bird and carried their prizes indoors uninjured. The housekeeper rescued the pigeons from the cats, and in return gave the wily hunters a nice slice of beef or mutton and a saucer of milk. Meanwhile, the pigeons were taken away, and after eating some corn and drinking some water, flew out of the window none the worse for their mauling by the cats.

STARS OF THE SILVER SCREEN

Animal behaviorists train cats for use in movies, television, and commercials. The cats learn to obey a variety of commands, such as sit and stay, go to a mark, move from A to B slowly, retrieve, jump, sit on a lap, and stare. As an actor, always bear in mind the old adage "never work with children or animals"—and some may add—especially cats, from their own bitter experience.

The first feline movie legend was Pepper, a gray alley cat, who turned up on set one day and was cast in many of the early Max Sennett silent movies alongside the megastars of the day—Charlie Chaplin and Fatty Arbuckle. However, when her favorite costar, Teddy the Great Dane, died, Pepper went into mourning and disappeared.

The leading role in Jake, *The Cat from Outer Space* (1978), was played by a professional feline actor named Rumple. If you look carefully when watching the early scenes, when Jake is demonstrating his illuminated collar's special powers, you may notice two thin electrical wires connected to the light-up collar running beside the cat.

In 1951, a talented but temperamental orange tabby, known as Orangey, played the title role in *Rhubarb*, a comedy movie about a cat that inherits a fortune. During filming, there weren't many laughs for the actor Ray Milland, Orangey's long-suffering costar. The cat took an immediate dislike to Mr. Milland, who had to be plastered with meat paste and sprayed with catnip just to keep the hostile feline near enough to complete the shoot.

Orangey went on to win a PATSY (Picture Animal Top Star of the Year, the equivalent of an Oscar for an animal actor) for his performance in *Rhubarb*—and Mr. Milland got nothing.

Ten years later, lucky old Orangey went on to play Cat— the "poor slob without a name"— opposite Audrey Hepburn as Holly Golightly in *Breakfast at Tiffany's* (1961). This time Miss Hepburn earned an Oscar nomination—and Orangey picked up another PATSY.

In the James Bond movies *You Only Live Twice* and *Diamonds Are Forever*, the part of the evil Ernst Stavro Blofeld's pampered Persian cat lounging on his lap was played by a fluffy white feline actor called Solomon.

In *Men in Black*, Orion the cat plays the guardian of a very important galaxy. A nasty cockroach kills his master and succeeds in stealing his galaxy because the MIB, played by Tommy Lee Jones and Will Smith, fail to arrest the cockroach in time. However, eventually they do destroy the cockroach and save the galaxy. Orion got good reviews for playing his role with great panache.

There was one small continuity glitch in *Men in Black*, which only the most observant would have noticed. When the cat is on the table in the diner, the name "Orion" on the cat's collar is spelled out in capital letters, but when it's on the table in the morgue, the word "Orion" is in calligraphy. The color of the cat's collar also seems to change between these two scenes.

One of the most popular movie cats, because of his numerous television appearances, is Spot— the first cat to boldly go where no cat had gone before. Spot and his master, the android Data, live on the starship *Enterprise*, which belonged to the United Federation of Planets. Obviously, Spot has many adventures— in his first movie *Generations*, the crashing of the Enterprise at the end almost cost him his life.

FAMOUS TELEVISION CATS

The little orange kitten seen meowing sweetly on the closing logo of the MTM Mary Tyler Moore Enterprises, Inc. TV Productions was played by Mimsey (1968–88) as a parody of the roaring Leo the Lion mascot that appeared at the beginning and end of the movie giant Metro-Goldwyn-Mayer's productions. She shot to stardom from a local animal shelter, then retired to live with an MTM employee in the San Fernando Valley.

Other programs produced by MTM used variations on the Mimsey Logo:

The Bob Newhart Show	Kitten meows normally as on The MTM Show
The Duck Factor	Instead of meowing, the kitten says, "Quack!"
Graham Kerr	Kitten wears a chef's hat
Hill Street Blues	Kitten wears a policeman's hat
Remington Steele	Kitten wears a Sherlock Holmes deerstalker cap and meerschaum pipe
St. Elsewhere	Kitten wears a surgical mask and smock
The Steve Allen Show	Kitten lip-syncs "Schmock!" in the voice of Steve Allen
The White Shadow	Kitten with black splotches dribbles a basketball

A reunion of the cast for *The Mary Tyler Moore Show* 20th Anniversary on February 18, 1991, ended with the kitten saying "Bye!" in Mary Tyler Moore's voice.

On the videos produced by MTM Home Video, the kitten holds a remote control, meows, hits rewind, and replays the kitten meowing.

In the final episode of *St. Elsewhere*, the poor little kitten is shown under the credits hooked up to a life-support monitor. As the show's credits reach their conclusion, the kitten flatlines.

FINICKY EATERS

The first Morris (1961–78) that acted as spokescat for 9Lives cat food, was a legend, possibly the greatest cat celebrity of all time in the United States. Morris' rise to stardom was a classic from rags to riches story. As a cute kitten in 1968, he was literally snatched from the jaws of death 20 minutes before he was to be euthanized at the Hinsdale Humane Society Animal Shelter in Lombard, Illinois. Bob Martwick, an animal talent scout and trainer, rescued him and named him Lucky.

In the advertisements for 9Lives cat food, Morris played the spoiled pampered pet, "the world's most finicky cat." When asked to choose between his favorite 9Lives and other cat foods, he was unerringly correct in his choice, throwing in a dismissive put-down for the alternatives available.

Known in the business as "the Clark Gable of cats"—whether for his good looks and acting style or his Rhett Butleresque "Frankly, my dear, I don't give a damn" approach to life is unclear. Morris number one also appeared in the movie *Shamus* (1973), alongside Burt Reynolds and Dyan Cannon.

> *"Hmph! Din-din. I'll eat when I'm ready."*
> THE VOICE OF MORRIS THE CAT

In 1972, the first Meow Mix cat food television commercial entitled Singing Cat featured a cute white-and-orange tabby singing the now immortal lyrics meow, meow, meow, meow . . . with subtitles translating what flavors the cat was asking for. A spokesperson for the ad agency later admitted that the shots of the cat singing were not strictly planned. Apparently, the cat was really choking on cat food while the advertisement was being recorded, and it was decided to dub music for a lip-sync effect afterward.

OTHER CAREERS

> *If the prospect of mousing for its livelihood doesn't appeal, there are many alternative career opportunities open to a cat.*

TASTE TESTERS: Pet food manufacturers often hire cats to test the palatability and appeal of their foods. When a food has been tested in a feeding trial it is usually stated on the label, giving consumers the reassurance that cats have actually eaten and liked the food they are buying.

BLOOD DONORS: To supply blood for cats in need of blood transfusions. Contact your local veterinary college or veterinarian for information on blood-donation programs.

THERAPISTS: Cats really are good for your health, lowering stress, reducing blood pressure, and adding to a general sense of well-being. More and more feline fanciers are sharing such benefits of pet power by having their cats registered as therapy cats to visit patients in hospitals and the elderly in nursing homes.

A cat named Manis is a favorite in an animal-therapy program at Selangor Cheshire Home in Malaysia. Children who have trouble walking will make astounding efforts to keep their balance so they can play with him.

COMPANION: Highly strung Thoroughbred horses often develop a strong attachment to another animal, such as a cat, which helps them to stay calm during the buildup to an important race.

🐾 Grimalkin was the beloved feline companion of the famous stallion Godolphin Arabian (1724–54), one of the founders of the modern Thoroughbred horse racing bloodstock. When the horse died, Grimalkin sat on his body until it was buried, then crept away and hid in a hayloft, where he died shortly afterward.

🐾 ASTROCAT: There have been few chances for cats to explore space. In fact, Félix was the first of only two cats that are known to have made space flights. The Soviet Union had already launched dogs, mice, monkeys, and apes into orbit before it sent a cat into space.

🐾 Originally a Paris street cat, after intensive training, on October 18, 1963, Félix was selected to be blasted off in a special capsule on top of a French *Véronique AG1* rocket, from the Colomb Bacar rocket base at Hammaguir in the Algerian Sahara. She traveled about 130 miles (210 km) into space, but didn't go into orbit before the capsule separated from the rocket and descended by parachute. The capsule and the astrocat were recovered safely. Unfortunately, what goes up doesn't always come down. There was another cat space flight on October 24, 1963, but that poor feline was never recovered.

🐾 CIRCUS CATS: A professional circus clown, Yuri Kuklachev started his unique Cat Theater in 1976 after coming across a kitten in a Moscow street. The show features a troupe of 30 talented cats performing amazing stunts—tightrope walking, ball balancing, handstands, running through mazes, and jumping from great heights. Kuklachev trains all the cats himself, according to their natural talents and characters.

🐾 CHURCH CATS: In Great Britain, there is a long tradition of church cats, which persists to this day. The most recent feline occupants of The Actor's Church, St. Paul's Church in Covent Garden, London, were called Inigo and Jones, after its architect and builder Inigo Jones (1573–1652).

CHAPTER 6

Amazing Powers

· ·

Survival is the name of the game in the animal kingdom, and

cats are great survivors. Equipped with highly tuned senses of

touch, hearing, sight, smell, and balance, which are vastly more

sensitive than our own, cats are constantly astounding us with

their powers of anticipation, It's as though they can predict events

of which we are oblivious until after they've happened, which can

be disconcerting. However, perhaps it's worth considering that the

cat's most amazing power of all is its ability to wheedle its way,

quickly, deeply, and permanently into the human heart.

A GREAT SENSE OF TIMING

There are times when cats seem possessed—and some might just leave it at that—of a sixth sense, a seemingly extrasensory perception that enables them to predict events, ranging from the everyday to the extraordinary to the downright catastrophic, with unerring accuracy. The most frequent manifestations of such apparently telepathic responses are a cat's anticipation of their owners returning home or going away; cats disappearing when their owners want to take them to the veterinarian; and cats that know when their owner is phoning home, even before the telephone is answered.

To some people, these powers are simply examples of cats using their keen intelligence, alertness, and hypersensitivities to put two and two together and come up with five. By picking up on subtle changes in their owners' body language, tone of voice, and regular habits, they can second-guess what is about to happen. To others, there has to be a more supernatural element involved in their amazing precognitive skills.

The French author Alexandre Dumas had a black-and-white cat called Mysouff ll that always seemed to know exactly when he would be coming home from work. Unfailingly, whether Dumas arrived at his usual time or later, the cat would meet him on the corner of the street and walk home with him. Dumas' mother would let Mysouff II out, but the cat always refused to leave the house if his master was running late.

Another remarkable example of feline timekeeping was reported from Switzerland. The cat's owner occasionally went to work for a friend in the Aargau canton. During these occasions, he rang home in the evening. One minute before this happened, the family cat always became restless and took up station next to the telephone. At other times, the man took the train to Biel and then rode home on his moped. On those days, the cat seemed to know and would go and sit outside the front door about 30 minutes before he arrived. Occasionally, the man arrived at Biel earlier than usual and phoned from the station. Once again the cat would sit near the telephone shortly before the call came in, then she would go to the front door. Although all these events happened very irregularly, inexplicably the cat seemed to know exactly where he was and what to expect after the calls.

There is a report of a cat called U-Boat, from a ship of unknown name, that loved to go on shore leave as soon as his ship reached port. Sometimes he was away for days, yet with a cat's uncanny instinct, he would always return just before sailing time. However, one day he misjudged his timing and missed roll call—so the ship had to get under way without him. As the crew looked back, they saw U-Boat running helter-skelter along the dock before making a death-defying leap onto the deck. To the delight of the crew, who were so pleased to have their good-luck mascot back safely, he landed successfully and promptly sat down to wash himself and regain his composure.

A scientist working at the British Antarctic Survey station on South Georgia in the Falklands in South America befriended a small female tabby cat, which he called Judith. Periodically, the little cat would put on some weight and disappear for a few weeks. When she turned up again, she would let the scientist follow her to see her kittens. Eventually, one of the scientist's colleagues drowned a litter of kittens and a distraught Judith vanished. Weeks, then months passed with no sign of the little tabby. However, one day the relief ship RRS *Bransfield* docked to transport the scientist back to his home. A nervous Judith seemed to know he was leaving the island and returned to the research center for one last visit. As the scientist reflected, it was as though the cat had come to say good-bye.

NO PLACE LIKE HOME

Reports of cats undertaking extraordinary journeys, covering hundreds of miles and many months, to be reunited with their human families appear from time to time. How they achieve such incredible feats of navigation without the aid of a satellite navigation system is still a mystery.

THE TOP TEN LONGEST TRAVELERS

1 TOM, 2,500 MILES (4,000 KM): When Mr. and Mrs. Charles Smith moved from St. Petersburg, Florida, to San Gabriel, California, in 1949, they left Tom behind to live in his old home with Robert Hanson, the new occupant. However, two weeks later, Mr. Hanson informed them that Tom had run away. Two years later, in August 1951, Mrs. Smith was disturbed by a cat howling in her yard. When Mr. Smith went outside to shoo it away, he couldn't believe his eyes—the cat that came running up to him was none other than the missing Tom. At first, Mrs. Smith doubted that it really could be Tom, but when she offered the cat a bowl of Pablum, Tom's favorite baby food, and he promptly licked it all up, she was convinced.

2 SUGAR, 1,500 MILES (2,400 KM): A two-year-old part-Persian cat, Sugar had a hip deformity that made it uncomfortable for her to travel by car. So, when her family moved from Anderson, California, to Gage, Oklahoma, her owners decided to leave her with a neighbor. However, two weeks after their departure, Sugar disappeared. Fourteen months later, Sugar turned up on her old owners' doorstep in Gage, having covered 100 miles (160 km) a month to reach a place she had never been to before.

3 MINOSCH, 1,485 MILES (2,400 KM): In 1981, Mehmet Tunc, a Turkish guest worker in Germany, took his family and his cat Minosch home for a vacation. Unfortunately, the cat disappeared at the Turkish border. The family returned to their home on the island of Sylt, in northern Germany without the cat—however, 61 days later, the family heard a faint scratching at the door, which turned out to be a scruffy Minosch.

4 SILKY, 1,472 MILES (2,370 KM): Ken Phillips lost Silky at Gin Gin, about 200 miles (320 km) north of Brisbane in Queensland, Australia, in the summer of 1977. However, on March 28, 1978, Silky reappeared at Mr. Phillips' house in a suburb of Melbourne. Apparently, the cat was as thin as a wisp and stank to high heaven.

5 KUZYA, 1,300 MILES (2,100 KM): In 2004, a two-year-old tomcat named Kuzya disappeared after the Efremov family took him with them from their home in the small village of Olenyok to the city of Yakutsk in eastern Russia for the summer. After failing to find him, the Efremovs had to go home without him. Yet, three months later Kuzya was discovered sitting on their doorstep in Olenyok, looking skinny and bedraggled. If the bites on his tail and his general cautiousness were anything to go by, his pilgrimage across the Yakutia republic, crossing Siberian woodland, hills, rivers, and lakes, was a traumatic one.

6 HOWIE, 1,200 MILES (1,900 KM): In 1978, a three-year-old Persian named Howie found his way home from the Gold Coast in Queensland, Australia, to Adelaide—a journey that took him a year. Although his white coat was matted and filthy and his paws were sore and bleeding, Howie was purring once he arrived home.

7 RUSTY, 950 MILES (1,500 KM): In 1949, an orange tomcat called Rusty traveled from Boston, Massachusetts, to Chicago, Illinois, in just 83 days. It is believed that he must have hitched rides on cars, trucks, or trains to cover the distance in such a record-breaking time.

8 GRINGO, 480 MILES (770 KM): The Servoz family's pet tomcat, Gringo, disappeared from their home in Lamarche-sur-Seine, France, in December 1982. The following July they discovered that he had relocated to their summer home in the French Riviera. Evidently wanting to escape the cold winter weather, he had made the journey south in a week and turned up at their home in the French Riviera, where neighbors took care of him.

9 MUDDY WATER WHITE, 450 MILES (725 KM): In June 1985, Muddy Water White jumped out of a van driven by his owner, Barbara Paule, in Dayton, Ohio. Almost exactly three years later, he arrived back home in Pennsylvania. She fed him for three days before even realizing that he was Muddy Water White, an identification that was later confirmed by the local veterinarian.

10 MURKA, 400 MILES (645 KM): In 1987, a stray cat, Murka, was adopted by Vladimir Donsov and his family in Moscow. Unfortunately, Murka abused their hospitality by killing the family's pet canaries. She was sent over 400 miles (645 km) away to Voronezh to live with Mr. Donsov's mother, but she vanished after two days. A year later, on October 19, 1989, Mr. Donsov stumbled across her in his Moscow apartment building, "dirty, hungry, pregnant, and minus the tip of her tail." This time she was allowed to stay.

*When moving to a new home,
always put the cat through the window
instead of the door, so that it will not leave.*

AMERICAN SUPERSTITION

MEDICAL ALERT

After being dumped in a river as a kitten, a black-and-white cat called Tee Cee was adopted by the Edmonds family in Sheffield, South Yorkshire, England. The grateful cat returned the favor by predicting when Michael Edmonds was about to have an epileptic seizure. Mr. Edmonds' fits used to be unexpected, but by adopting Tee Cee, the family gained an early warning system. They noticed that the cat would sit and stare at Mr. Edmonds just before he was about to have a fit, then run to alert Mrs. Edmonds. While Mr. Edmonds was experiencing a fit, Tee Cee stayed close until he regained consciousness.

In 2007, Sylvester, an orange, part-Persian cat, probably saved his 90-year-old owner's life when he alerted neighbors that something was wrong by meowing at their door. The neighbors were smart enough to realize that this was strange behavior for Sylvester, who was normally standoffish. Initially, they thought that the cat was hungry and called Sylvester's owner on the telephone, but the line was busy, so they assumed everything was okay. Later on, when they saw that Sylvester's owner had not put out her garbage, they called her once again—but her telephone line was still busy. The neighbors walked around the house calling for the woman. When they failed to get any reply, they called the police. Officers found the woman stuck in her bath, suffering from hypothermia, and called an ambulance to take her to hospital, where she recovered.

In 2005, in Columbus, Ohio, Gary Rosheisen fell out of his wheelchair. He wasn't wearing his medical-alert necklace and was unable to get up or call for help himself. Nevertheless, police received an emergency call from Rosheisen's home telephone, but could hear nobody on the line. After calling back and getting no answer they went to the apartment to investigate. The policemen found Gary lying on his bedroom floor, and they came across his orange-and-tan striped cat, Tommy, sitting next to the telephone on the floor in the living room. According to the police, the only plausible explanation was that the amazing Tommy dialed the emergency number, probably using the speed dial button on the telephone. Rosheisen wasn't surprised. He got the cat three years ago to help lower his blood pressure and he'd once attempted to train Tommy to dial 911.

WARNING! WARNING!

A heroic eight-week-old kitten named Tinny saved a family of four from a fire in their home in the early hours of the morning on December 2006, in Brinsmead, Cairns, Queensland, Australia. By meowing loudly and scratching the face of 14-year-old Zac, who was sleeping on a burning mattress, the kitten alerted the family to the fire. This early warning allowed them enough time to escape the flames. The kitten's early intervention not only saved the family, but also spared their home from major damage. Meg, the family's dog, proved not to be such a reliable rescue hero—the dog only started barking when the fire engines arrived. Zac's mom, Marina, who had given the kitten to her daughter Chaniece as an early Christmas present only four weeks earlier, said the little cat was "worth its weight in Whiskas."

A family cat, Shadow, helped to save the lives of Karen, her two young sons, and the family dog Duke on the night of January 16, 2003. The cat's loud, persistent meowing woke Karen, who was sleeping in the basement bedroom.

> *I have studied many philosophers and many cats.*
> *The wisdom of cats is infinitely superior.*
>
> HIPPOLYTE TAINE (1828–93), FRENCH HISTORIAN

Feeling sick and dizzy, Karen soon realized something was wrong. She dialed 911 immediately and then got everyone out of the house. The family members were all experiencing carbon monoxide poisoning and had to be treated at a nearby hospital. Later, firefighters detected CO levels as high as 300 parts per million at the residence, resulting from a faulty furnace, a situation that could have ended in tragedy but did not, in part because of Shadow's warnings.

At 6:46 in the morning of June 14, 1998, in Quebec, Canada, Guylaine Labonté's cat, Étoile de Nuit, began meowing loudly. Thinking nothing of it, Guylaine tried to go back to sleep, but the persistent feline was determined to wake her owner. Groggy and sleepy-eyed, Guylaine arose to find a fire raging in her bathroom and smoke swirling about her living room. Guylaine rushed to wake her neighbors, but when she returned to get Étoile de Nuit, the cat had disappeared. As the fire continued to spread, Guylaine searched frantically for Étoile de Nuit, but she was forced to flee the building as it burned to the ground. Much to Guylaine's relief, a very frightened Étoile de Nuit was later seen by a police officer close to the ashes of the building. Étoile de Nuit really was a star that night.

At 4:00 in the morning on Monday, May 14, 2002, Mona Melanson was sleeping so deeply in her Châteauguay apartment, also in Quebec, Canada, that she didn't hear the fire alarm. Fortunately, her four-year-old cat, Beau, started hurling himself against the closed bedroom door, which woke up his owner. Still groggy, Mona got up to see what all the commotion was about. When she opened her bedroom door, she was horrified to find that her apartment was engulfed in such thick smoke that she couldn't see to the end of the hallway. Mona and Beau had no choice but to run out onto the second-floor balcony and wait in terror until the Châteauguay Fire Department rescued them both.

Hobbes, a five-year-old orange tabby cat helped save the life of his owner Sheri Coull by waking her up late one night because her apartment in St. Thomas, Ontario, Canada, was on fire. Sheri's smoke detector had failed to go off, but Hobbes' persistent yowling woke the household, enabling the occupants to get out of the apartment building before it was engulfed in smoke and fumes.

A seaman serving on the Norwegian-flag tanker *Rona Star* adopted a stray kitten in Mina Al Ahmadi in 1965, and the animal took up residence in the radio room. From then on it refused to set foot on shore, despite being carried down the gangway onto the land many times. That is until the night of June 15, 1965, when the *Rona Star* was in wet dock at Rotterdam's Verolme shipyard, undergoing cleaning. It was on that date when the cat became extremely agitated, meowing and howling. It left the radio room, scooted down the gangway, and disappeared. No sooner had the animal reached the shore than the ship exploded in a ball of fire and 16 people were killed. The seaman who adopted the cat never saw it again.

BOMB ALERT

In the Blitz in London, England, when the city was being bombarded by bombs during World War II, there are stories of cats having saved the lives of whole families who, seeing their cats dashing to the shelters, would follow, reaching safety just before the bombs started to fall.

A cat nicknamed Bomber could tell the difference between the sounds of British Royal Air Force planes and German aircraft from a long way off, making him a marvelous early warning system for his human companions.

As an important manufacturing center in the West Midlands of England, Coventry was heavily bombed by the German Luftwaffe in 1940. Gladys Steer, a young girl living in the city at the time, later recalled how her cat would always go and sit at the top of the basement steps a couple of minutes before the air-raid warning siren sounded, giving the family extra time to take shelter in the basement before the bombs started falling.

One cat, named Andrew, was the mascot of the Allied Forces Mascot Club during World War II. He could tell when a bomb was going to strike nearby. When Andrew went for cover, everyone around him knew it was time to duck.

During World War II, a cat named Faith adopted St. Augustine's Church in London, England, as her home. The pastor, Father Henry Ross, and the congregation took the feline to their hearts. Faith had a kitten in 1940, which the worshippers decided to name Panda. One day, for no obvious reason as far as they could see, Faith moved Panda out of the warm church and down into the cold basement—and no matter how much cajoling they tried, Faith would not bring her kitten back up into the warmth of the church. The next night the area was bombarded by air raids and, unfortunately, the church was extensively damaged. However, Faith and young Panda survived as bombs exploded around them. Her devotion and bravery became well known throughout London, and served as an inspiration to many people through the dark days of the war.

WEATHER FORECASTING— OR FORE-CATSING

In the 1930s, there was a white tomcat named Napoleon living in Baltimore, Maryland. His owner, Mrs. de Shields, noted that every time it was about to rain Napoleon would lie on the floor, stretch out his front legs, and tuck his head down between them. During one particular year, there was a drought that had lasted for over a month, until one day Mrs. de Shields noticed Napoleon taking up his rain-approaching pose. However, according to the official local forecast, the weather wasn't about to break. Mrs. de Shields put her trust in Napoleon and telephoned a newspaper, telling them that it was going to rain because her cat had predicted it. Lo and behold, it did rain! After that, Napoleon's premonitions were published in the newspaper. When he died, his tombstone was inscribed Napoleon the Weather Prophet 1917–36. In the six years that Napoleon made his predictions, he never got the weather wrong—a record envied by most human meteorologists.

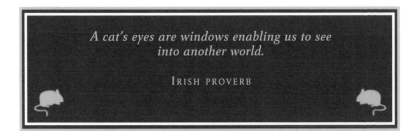

A cat's eyes are windows enabling us to see into another world.

IRISH PROVERB

CAT SUPERSTITIONS ABOUT WEATHER

Cat on its brain, it's going to rain.

If a cat washes behind its ears, rain is coming.

When a cat licks its tail, a storm is coming.

If a cat lies curled up with the flat part of the top of its head on the ground, it's going to rain.

When a cat stares out of a sunny window all day, rain is on the way.

When a cat sleeps with all four paws tucked underneath its body, bad weather is coming.

According to sailors, if a cat licks its fur against the way in which it laid, a hailstorm was coming.

If the cat turns her tail to the fire, there will be a hard frost.

A cat sitting with its back to the fire indicates a storm is on the way.

If a cat sneezes, then rain is on the way.

A cat sharpening its claws on a table leg signals a change in the weather, usually for the better.

In China, a winking cat warns that it will start raining soon.

When a cat jumps up onto a shelf or beam, country people swear that high water is on the way.

NATURAL DISASTERS

As of yet, there is no man-made instrument that can predict when or where an earthquake will occur until the ground starts trembling. However, it seems that animals, including cats, can detect when a big earthquake is coming about three hours before the shaking begins. How cats register an imminent earthquake—or a volcanic eruption or intense electric storm—is still uncertain. They may be supersensitive to the tiniest tremors that go undetected by monitoring equipment or to the dramatic buildup of static electricity that precedes earthquakes, or they may be particularly responsive to upheavals in the earth's magnetic field that accompany earthquakes. Possibly all three reactions occur at once.

🐾 The Chinese have long believed cats are able to foretell quakes. In 1975, the city of Haicheng was evacuated days in advance of a devastating earthquake, which measured 7.3 on the Richter scale—based on the agitated behavior of the local cats and dogs. An estimated 150,000 lives were saved.

🐾 In the early evening of May 6, 1976, people in the Friuli-Venezia Giulia region of northeastern Italy were bemused to see their cats going berserk, running about wildly, scratching to get out of the house, and vanishing when outside. However, at 9:00 p.m. a violent earthquake hit the area, killing nearly 1,000 people and causing hundreds of millions of dollars worth of damage to local property.

🐾 In 1989, completely out of character, a cat living in Santa Cruz, California, started behaving as if it was scared and disappeared up into the attic just three hours before a massive earthquake hit the area.

🐾 It's thought that about one-third of the cats in the area picked up the Great Hanshin earthquake in Japan in 1995, which demolished the city of Kobe and killed over 6,000 people.

🐾 After the earthquake off the coast of Sumatra in 2005 that launched a killer tsunami across the Indian Ocean, the Thais found that not a single animal was killed by the wave. They came to the conclusion that the animals must have been able to tell that an earthquake was about to happen and fled to safety.

🐾 One night in March 1944, a cat called Toto, which lived with a family in the shadow of Mount Vesuvius, Italy, woke his owner by scratching urgently at his face. Hardly surprisingly, the man was not pleased but he couldn't make the cat go away. Then it occurred to his wife that perhaps Toto was trying to warn them that Vesuvius was about to erupt. They hastily left the area, only an hour before the volcano exploded, spewing out red-hot molten lava that engulfed their house and killed 30 people.

> *There are no ordinary cats.*
>
> COLETTE (1873–1954)
> FRENCH NOVELIST

INSTINCT FOR DEATH

🐾 In ancient Greece, a cat was believed to be a psychopomp—a sage that waited with a dying person, comforting their soul and escorting it across into the afterlife at the moment of death.

🐾 A slightly different version of this belief occurred in ancient Thailand, where it was believed that when a very spiritual person died, their soul entered the body of a cat, and then went to heaven when the cat died.

🐾 Oscar is not just your average two-year-old tabby-and-white cat. As a kitten, he joined the nursing team on the third-floor advanced dementia unit of the Steere House Nursing and Rehabilitation Center in Providence, Rhode Island, in 2005. Since then, this remarkable cat has accurately predicted and attended the deaths of more than 25 patients in the final stages of Alzheimer's, Parkinson's, stroke, and dementia. Every morning he does a ward round to assess the condition of each patient. As death approaches, Oscar returns to curl up on the dying patient's bed, purring for the last few hours of that person's life. The compassionate feline is particular about the timing and being there at the end, and he will wail outside the door if he is excluded. He ignores patients who may be dying soon, but not that day. The nursing staff have come to respect his judgement. His assessment of the imminence of death gives them time to call in the patient's family so they can gather at the bedside to say their final farewells. Exactly how Oscar knows precisely when a patient will die is not clear, but there is speculation that he uses his acute sense of smell to pick up on chemical changes in metabolism as death draws near, of which the medical staff is unaware.

🐾 In 2007, nurses at another nursing home, in Seattle, Oregon, also reported having a cat that had the mysterious power of being able to tell when a resident was about to die. During his three years at the retirement home, the 10-year-old tabby, named Buckwheat, is said to have kept about 36 patients company in the final hours of their life, comforting the dying person by climbing up on the bed and curling up next to him or her.

Penny, a three-year-old cat, established an extraordinarily close relationship with her owner, Bernard Marks, during the last few months of his owner's life, as he was dying of cancer in the summer of 2005. In fact, this relationship was so close that the two companions died within seconds of each other at Marks' home in Hudson in New Hampshire. As Bernard declined, Penny also got sicker; when he took his last breath, the cat meowed in pain, and her body contorted before she collapsed and died.

RECOVERY ROOM

A tiny blind cat called Peanut, but affectionately nicknamed Peanutter, comforted animal patients at the Heartland Veterinary Hospital in Kentucky. In spite of being blind, Peanut could sense when another animal needed her help. After a patient came out of surgery, she slipped into its cage to snuggle up close. Sometimes she even groomed the unconscious animal. Then just before or as soon as the patient woke, Peanut left. On one occasion, all was not going too well for a ten-year-old golden retriever, Rajah, who had surgery to remove a large tumor and a second operation to stop the bleeding. When Rajah's owner went to visit her sick pet she found Peanut lying beside the dog, her front legs stretched out, as if hugging Rajah's neck. Although still heavily sedated, Rajah seemed to be soothed by Peanut's purring. Peanut stayed with Rajah for about three hours, licking the dog's ears and head. It was all the more amazing because normally Rajah couldn't stand cats and was always chasing or growling at them. However, even when the anesthetic wore off, Rajah calmly sniffed and rubbed noses with Peanut—and went on to make a good recovery.

CHAPTER 7

Cats Do the Darndest Things

As expert hunters, cats naturally poke their noses into every nook and cranny in search of prey and give cosy corners a whisker-tip frisking to find sheltered snoozing spots. Such insatiable nosiness may be one of the cat's most endearing qualities, but, to paraphrase an old adage, that curiosity can come close to killing it at times. Tales of cats whose innocent explorations and more impetuous moments have escalated into life-threatening adventures are legion. Fortunately, cats have a phenomenal will to survive, coupled with an amazing ability to endure privation and bounce back once rescued.

GOING UP

Sometimes it's necessary to resort to unceremonious measures to dislodge stubborn cats that refuse to be lured down from lengthy vigils in the branches of a tree. One calico cat resolutely resisted all enticements to come down from its perch 60 feet (18 m) up in a willow tree for a week. The time came to call in the Yonkers Fire Department in New York. Their ladders were not long enough to reach where the cat was perched, so they arrived with their high-pressure water hose. The second blast was lucky, and they succeeded in knocking the cat out of the tree and catching it in a safety sheet stretched out below. Treetop, as the cat had become known, was drenched but otherwise unharmed.

In January 2006, a kitten called Smirnoff climbed up a chimney flue in her home in Penzance, Great Britain, and refused to come down. After she'd spent five days up there without anything to eat or drink, everybody was desperate to get her out. The fire department was called in and eventually one exasperated fireman started barking at her like

a dog. That got Smirnoff moving within reach of the rescuers.

On February 28, 1980, a female cat climb up the textured outside wall of an apartment in Bradford, England—about 70 feet (21 m) of it. This miraculous feat was performed so that the cat could escape from a not-so-friendly dog.

In Gulfport, Mississippi, during Hurricane George in 1998, a cat called Big Boy was blown onto the roof of a store, then fell 60 feet (18 m) into an oak tree. In May 2001, he was still in the tree—he had been eating and sleeping in the tree, and climbed from branch to branch for exercise.

It's rare for a cat to get firmly wedged in a tree but that's exactly what happened to one poor black cat, who was later nicknamed Forest. One morning two boys in their backyard in Massachusetts heard a cat meowing from deep in the wood. They didn't think much of it at the time, but when they heard the meowing again later on in the afternoon, the two friends decided to investigate. The boys came across a stray black cat stuck about 5 feet (1.5 m) above the ground in the fork between two tree trunks. Eventually, members of the fire department had to use power tools to save the wedged cat. Within minutes, the tree trunks were spread and the cat was freed. After medical treatment, the lucky cat lived to climb another tree.

Cats are fearless climbers, but none has ever climbed higher than a four-month-old kitten belonging to Josephine Aufdenblatten of Geneva, Switzerland. During the summer of 1950, the adventurous feline followed a group of mountaineers, led by Edmund Biner, 14,691 feet (4,478 m) up the Matterhorn, the tallest mountain in the Alps in Europe. On the first day, it climbed up to a hut at 12,500 feet (3,810 m), where it spent the night. The group continued, along with the kitten, until they eventually reached the summit. The climbers were amazed that, although the little cat slipped several times, it always managed to regain its footing and keep up with them. The determined kitten was there to share in the celebrations of conquering the peak. When the group descended the mountain, instead of using its own paw power to return home, the kitten hitched a lift down in the backpack of one of the mountain guides.

COMING DOWN

As many a cat who has suffered the indignity of getting stuck up a tree can report, its needle-sharp claws are well designed for the going-up part; however, they are less suited to coming down, when they offer much less grip. If ever called upon to advise a cat on making its descent from a tree, always suggest it slithers down backward.

Cats have an inbuilt automatic twisting reaction and, given enough time, are able to twist their bodies around to land feet first. However, if falling from too low a height, a tree perhaps, a cat won't have enough time to twist around and can't land feet downward. If it falls from too great a height, it's unlikely to survive whether it lands on its feet or not—and even if the cat lives, it will certainly receive serious injuries.

According to a delightful legend, the cat was endowed with its ability to land safely on its feet by the prophet Mohammed. Summoned to prayer one day while his best-loved cat, Muezza, was sleeping on his sleeve, Mohammed cut off his sleeve to avoid disturbing the cat's slumbers. On returning, the cat bowed to thank him for his thoughtfulness. As a reward for the cat's gratitude and good manners,

Mohammed granted cats the ability to land feet down after every fall.

The luckiest cat alive has to be Andy, who belonged to Senator Ken Myers from Florida. In the 1970s, he fell about 200 feet (61 m) from the sixteenth floor of an apartment building—and lived! His great good fortune landed him in the record books, too, as the survivor of the longest nonfatal fall in cat history.

Another lucky cat was named Shiva. She plunged 60 feet (18 m) from her fifth-floor apartment, yet managed to survive. One moment she was on the windowsill, the next she was leaping through an open window after passing birds and plummeting to the ground. Her owner searched frantically for Shiva, but she didn't turn up until the following day, limping but alive and well. X-rays showed that she had escaped with just a broken shoulder and front leg. Apparently, Shiva looked more traumatized after spending the night out in the rain than by her fall.

THREE-LEGGED WONDER

Some cats land on their feet in more ways than one—even if, in this case, the cat had only three legs. A filthy, scared, and feisty alley cat living on the streets of Kabul, Afghanistan, had one of his hind legs crushed by a car. His heavy-metal meowing attracted the attention and sympathies of two American journalists, who eventually managed to catch him and take him to the Afghan Stray Animal League, a charity helping stray animals in the war-torn capital, where his injured leg was amputated. Unfortunately, Mr. Stumpy, as he became known, ran away after the operation and, by the time he was found again, his wound was seriously infected. It took over a month of painful daily bandage changes to save Mr. Stumpy, who gradually turned into a sociable, friendly little cat.

The charity caring for him found someone in the United States willing to adopt him. And that is how, in the summer of 2004, Mr. Stumpy traveled to the United States to live with Bryan Wockley and his family in the Washington, D.C., area, where he learned to climb tall trees on three legs—and his loud, insistent meow was recognized far and wide.

TRAPPED!

🐾 A hunting cat got more than it bargained for when it pushed its head into an empty glass jar to get at a mouse inside and got stuck. A motorist found the bewildered cat wandering beside a road with the jar over its head and a mouse cowering just beyond its nose and took it to a police station. Several police officers tried tugging and twisting the jar, but they failed to free the cat or the mouse. In the end, the cat found the solution by smashing the jar on the floor—and the mouse ran off.

🐾 Normally, a cat would not choose a freezing cold place to settle down, but Louis, a cat belonging to the Honer family in Oklahoma City, had little choice. He had been missing for four weeks, when Todd Honer decided to clean out an old refrigerator in his barn. As he opened the door, out fell an emaciated Louis, weighing just three pounds (1.4 kg). It turned out that four-year-old Tyce Honer had managed to shut the once 10-pound (4.5 kg) cat in the refrigerator in the barn "to keep it safe."

🐾 In October 2006, a woman accidentally posted a cat in the package she was sending to her nephew for his birthday. Edith Schonberg, 67, from Rosdorf in Schleswig-Holstein, Germany, posted the package without noticing that her three-year-old tomcat Felix had crawled inside for a nap. Her oversight was only noticed when a mailman separating the mail heard the package meowing and called the police. Felix's owner hadn't even noticed the tomcat was missing until the police called. Edith thought he'd been snoozing all the time and reckoned that Felix must have found his way into the package while she was searching for some tape to finish wrapping it.

🐾 In 2007, on the day that the Duke family was due to move from Kent in the south of England to Inverness in Scotland, they couldn't find their 14-year-old cat Lucy anywhere. Eventually, the heartbroken family had to take a taxi to the airport without her. To their surprise, seven weeks later the Dukes got a call from the man who'd bought their house saying that he'd found a weak Lucy under the floorboards in the kitchen. She'd lost more than 2 pounds (1 kg) and was severely dehydrated—the veterinarian reckoned she must have survived by licking condensation from underfloor pipes. Lucy eventually recovered and was reunited with her delighted family.

🐾 A statue of Queen Victoria in Canterbury, New Zealand, was unveiled on May 25, 1903. However, a few days after the statue was installed cries of a distressed cat were heard emanating from inside. Before the statue had been erected, it had lain on the ground and a cat had evidently slipped inside the hollow figure. So Queen Victoria had to be ignominiously hoisted off her pedestal while the cat was enticed out with a tasty fish.

🐾 In September 2007, creeping into a little nook almost cost one young cat his life—he nearly became a permanent part of a high school in Georgia. During the building of a flight of concrete stairs, the curious feline decided it was the ideal place to investigate. Luckily, one of the construction workers heard the kitten meowing near the new staircase. It seems that Stone, as he's now known, had crawled under the framework for the stairs before the concrete was poured in and got trapped within the setting mortar. The drying concrete had to be drilled away before a stiff kitten could be rescued. The concrete-covered kitten had to be shaved clean, but at least his fur grew back.

BRAVE CATS

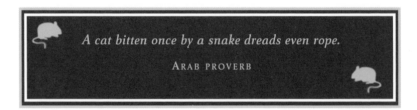

On July 27, 2003, in Dorval, Quebec, Canada, Kimberley Kotar was in her garden when she came face to face with a snake. Only inches away, hissing and shaking its tail, the viper was ready to strike Kimberly. However, her cat Sosa dashed to the rescue, lashing out at the snake. It was just as well the brave little cat intervened. The snake, which was later identified as a highly poisonous eastern cottonmouth, is not native to Quebec. If Kimberley had been bitten, she might have died because there is no antidote serum readily available in the province. Although Sosa was bitten in the paw in the process, miraculously, the brave cat managed to pull through after three days in an animal hospital.

A cat bitten once by a snake dreads even rope.

ARAB PROVERB

In the cleanup operation after the collapse of the twin towers of the World Trade Center on September 11, 2001, there were many tales of bravery and survival against the odds. Beneath the rubble where the World Trade Center had once stood, rescuers were delighted to discover one resourceful cat, curled up in a carton of napkins in a forgotten basement. When the box was brought up into the daylight, there were found to be even more survivors inside—three newborn kittens. Amid the mayhem, the mother cat had managed to pick out one of the few safe places in which to give birth to her family. Mom was christened Hope and the kitties were called Freedom, Amber, and Flag.

On a freezing March night in 1996, an extraordinary demonstration of feline motherly love above and beyond the call of duty was played out in

Brooklyn, New York. A stray calico cat—later known as Scarlett—was living in an empty garage when fire broke out. The New York Fire Department arrived on the scene to put out the fire. While the firefighters were extinguishing the blaze, they noticed a cat going in and out of the inferno. The courageous mother was rescuing her kittens and carried all six of her four-week-old kittens to safety. She managed to perform this feat even though she was fighting for breath and had already been severely injured—her eyelids were blistered shut, her ears were burned raw, and her paws and coat were singed. A firefighter immediately rushed the mother cat and her kittens to the North Shore Animal Clinic in Port Washington, Long Island, where veterinarians battled to save Scarlett and her family. Unfortunately, the weakest kitten didn't survive; however, after many weeks of tender care, Scarlett and her remaining five kittens were nursed back to health and they were all found homes.

When Bonnie the cat found two men stealing pet food from her owner's warehouse, she attacked the burglars. The hapless pair made their escape with only a few bags of loot loaded into their van.

Amazingly, Jack, a small orange tabby living with Donna Dickey and her family in West Milford, New Jersey, proved more than a match for a black bear when it strayed into the family's backyard. The terrified trespasser was forced up a tree—not once, but twice—by a hissing Jack, and could only manage to escape when Ms. Dickey called her pet back into the house.

SOME LIKE IT HOT!

It's just as well that cats like to be a lot warmer than humans. People feel uncomfortable when their skin gets warmer than 112°F (44.5°C), but cats don't start to feel the heat until their skin temperature reaches 126°F (52°C).

In 2007, Sunny was lucky to be alive after getting baked in the afternoon sun. He'd been packed into a duffel bag full of clothes that was left beside a dumpster outside an apartment complex in Lynnwood, Washington. Fortunately, the six-month-old black-and-white kitten had enough breath left to cry out and catch the attention of someone passing by. When found, Sunny had heatstroke. His body temperature was 107°F (41.7°C)—normally a cat's body temperature is 100.5–102.5°F (38–39°C). Happily, the dehydrated kitten rallied after being cooled down and hooked up to intravenous fluids and was soon purring his gratitude at the rescue center.

In March 1999, Talbot, a six-month-old stray cat wandered into the Peugeot car plant in Ryton, England, and went to sleep in the car body shell of a Peugeot 206 on the assembly line. The shell went into the paint-baking oven at a temperature of 145°F (62.7°C), with the cat still asleep inside. The workers noticed him half an hour later when the shell emerged and used a hose to cool the cat down. Unbelievably he survived, although his four paw pads were completely burned off and his fur was singed.

According to the Californian Pasadena Fire Department, in January 2004, a pet cat managed to set his owner's house on fire by knocking over a lamp in the bedroom. The lamp, which was on at the time, was believed to have fallen

> *We should be careful to get out of an experience only the wisdom that is in it—and stop there; lest we be like the cat that sits down on a hot stove-lid. She will never sit down on a hot stove-lid again—and that is well; but also she will never sit down on a cold one anymore.*
>
> FROM *PUDD'NHEAD WILSON'S NEW CALENDAR*
> MARK TWAIN (1835–1910), AMERICAN AUTHOR

onto a chair and set the upholstery on fire. Although the fire damaged other furniture in the bedroom and caused smoke damage throughout the house, it was contained in the one room and didn't cause any structural damage. And the feline arsonist managed to escape from the flames unscathed.

Steve Yingling, a resident of South Lake Tahoe, California, had a wonderful surprise when he was finally able to return to his home destroyed by the Angora Fire in the summer of 2007. He found his 15-year-old cat, Kit Cat, hiding in a metal damper at the bottom of the chimney. She was a bit groggy and her paws were burned, but apart from that, the feline seemed little the worse for wear.

In the summer of 2007, a cat in New Jersey was incredibly lucky to survive a house on fire by hiding in a couch. Stunned firefighters in West Orange found the cat after they had spent 30 minutes extinguishing the blaze, which had gutted the home.

In March 1999, a tabby cat wandered into an electricity substation in Hull, England, and received an 11,000-volt electric shock. A Yorkshire Electricity engineer saw him and managed to carry him clear of a 132,000-volt live terminal. The cat was given the nickname Sparky and became a local celebrity. Although he had burned paws, singed fur and whiskers, and paralyzed ears, Sparky was extremely lucky to have survived an electric shock of that magnitude, which would more than likely have killed a human being. Bizarrely, Sparky couldn't keep away from the substation and suffered another massive electric shock later on the same year. Unfortunately, the second shock killed him.

HITCHHIKERS

Some cats travel to be reunited with their owners (see pages 92–94), but others travel because they manage to get themselves stuck in a difficult situation.

🐾 A six-week-old kitten traveled 300 miles (480 km) from Jackson, New Jersey, to Kingston, New York—under a car. Her adventure started at a camping resort in September 2007. As a couple were packing to leave, they thought they heard a cat meowing but didn't investigate. They eventually parked outside a store in Kingston, alongside a car with a dog inside. The dog began barking at their car, then a kitten started howling. They looked underneath the car and found a kitten under the spare tire. When the kitten, dubbed Jersey, was lifted out, it was uninjured, despite traveling so close to the road.

🐾 During a 900-mile (1,450-km) drive from Avellino in the Campania region of Italy to the Austrian capital Vienna, Vincenzo Frustaci was disturbed by a squeaking coming from the front of his car. When he arrived at his destination, he asked a mechanic to examine the car; a kitten was discovered hiding in the fender.

🐾 Since January 2007, bus drivers on a bus route from Walsall to Wolverhampton, in England, have observed a white tomcat wearing a purple collar running to catch their bus at a particular bus stop. Two or three times a week, after traveling 440 yards (402 m), Macavity—as they named him—gets off at the next stop, which just happens to be located near a food establishment that specializes in fish. Macavity has never been seen catching the bus back.

🐾 This hitchhiker hitched a ride in a boat instead of a car. A Florida fisherman found a tabby cat treading water in the middle of the Rocky Bayou, bobbing up and down among swimmers and jet skiers. At first, he thought it was an otter, but then he realized it was a cat swimming about 200 yards (185 m) from land. He hauled the cat onboard in a landing net. The cat was overjoyed to be out of the water and seemed comfortable on a boat. He sailed ashore, happily ensconced on a cushion in the bow.

OVERSEAS TRAVELERS

🐾 Emily the cat disappeared from her home in Appleton, Wisconsin, at the end of September 2005. On October 24, she turned up in Nancy, France, when the container she had somehow got into was delivered to its destination. The cat was identified by the tag on the collar around her neck. Emily stayed in France for a few months. In December, Continental Airlines found her a seat in business class for a comfortable flight back to the United States. According to the airline steward who served her during the flight, Emily had acquired a taste for French cat food and didn't touch the salmon Continental offered her.

🐾 In April 2002, an overly curious cat called Top Cat unexpectedly ended up in Bordeaux, France, after climbing into a moving van that was transporting items from a neighbor's home in St. Neot, Cornwall, in Great Britain, to the French city. Due to the quarantine laws in Great Britain, Top Cat could not return home straight away. His owner, Jayne Manley, took a ferry to Santander in northern Spain, where she was reunited with her truant cat. She then traveled, with Top Cat safely in a basket, to Malaga in southern Spain, where her cat had to spend seven months living with a friend. This allowed him to get a pet passport, so he could return to Cornwall without being in quarantine for months.

🐾 One cat made the trip from China among the china! She seems to have chosen a crate of crockery for a peaceful snooze, blissfully unaware that it was about to be loaded onto a ship bound for Great Britain. Late in May 2006, the crate, with cat inside, was finally delivered to a firm in Nottinghamshire in central England. Chairman Miaow, as she became known, must have subsisted on a diet of cardboard and condensation for the 26 days the cargo was en route from China.

MORE OVERSEAS TRAVELERS

🐾 Chinese cats are obviously pretty stalwart. Another cat from China survived for 30 days in a container being transported to Tampa, Florida. On release, the feline was dehydrated and skinny, weighing only 3 pounds (1.4 kg). However, Norman Goldberg, who opened the container, said that in other respects she seemed remarkably well.

🐾 The owner of the Olympia Moto Sports store in Hendersonville, North Carolina, was amazed to find a small furry stowaway when he received delivery of a consignment of motorcycle equipment in May 2004. Store staff first noticed a foul smell when they opened the crate, then saw something moving. Shining a forklift's headlights into the crate, they discovered a weak and terrified tabby cat. It's thought that the cat, now called China, chewed its way into a cardboard box in a crate, which was then bolted shut and loaded onto a ship that left Shanghai on April 3. Amazingly, the cat had survived a 35-day journey from China to the United States trapped in a cargo crate without food or water.

🐾 One cat, who earned himself the name of Costco, apparently had enough of sunny California. The four-month-old kitten stowed away on a cargo ship, which sailed 3,000 miles (4,800 km) from the West Coast to Kauai, Hawaii. When Costco employees in Lihue, Kauai, unpacked a mixed dry goods container, they found the distraught kitten, who had spent at least a week as cargo. After setting off the motion sensor alarms in the warehouse all night, Costco was eventually captured. Apparently, Costco soon recovered from his adventures and enjoyed the laid-back pace of island life while he was in quarantine.

🐾 Spice's owner was about to move from Hawaii to California and was packing a huge shipping container with household goods. Unfortunately, unknown to her, her three-year-old calico cat had somehow managed to get inside. Before Spice could make an escape, the container was sealed up and heading toward California on the high seas. Spice's owner was worried when she couldn't find her cat; however, she had to catch her flight and so she asked the neighbors to look out for Spice. Meanwhile, Spice spent 18 days in the dark container without food or water. When her owner opened the container she noticed cat hair on the floor. When she started removing items, she saw a frightened Spice poking her head out from behind one of the bicycles.

🐾 Although they had not been previously renowned for their sentimentality, some of the dock workers from the Newton King Tanker Terminal at the port of Taranaki on North Island, New Zealand, were willing to move heaven and earth for the return of the wharf's friendly nine-year-old calico cat, known as Colin's. The feline had gone AWOL aboard a methanol tanker that was heading for Yeosu, South Korea, in November 2001. Apparently, the charming Colin's got into deep water when she enticed a South Korean sailor to take her onboard for some food. Unfortunately, the ship departed while the pair were busy catnapping after the cat's feast. After two weeks, a 6,000-mile (9,660-km) voyage, and a major mercy mission, Colin's was finally reunited with the terminal superintendent, Gordon MacPherson, when the ship docked in Yeosu. The two companions flew home together in style on a Korean Airlines Boeing 747.

UP, UP, AND AWAY

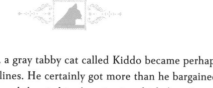

On October 15, 1910, a gray tabby cat called Kiddo became perhaps one of the first airborne felines. He certainly got more than he bargained for when he stowed away onboard the airship *America*, in which American explorer Walter Wellman (1858–1934) and five companions planned to cross the Atlantic Ocean. After taking off from Atlantic City, New Jersey, Kiddo made it clear that he didn't enjoy flying by meowing and howling loudly and incessantly. Eventually, the first engineer, Melvin Vaniman, couldn't stand the cat's protestations any longer and radioed for help. However, plans to lower Kiddo into a boat below the airship had to be abandoned because of bad weather. The unlucky cat had to stay onboard the craft, but he soon regained his equanimity. As it turned out, Kiddo proved more useful than a barometer at giving advanced warning of bad weather ahead. In fact, the navigator, Murray Simon, went so far as to suggest that no future airship flight across the Atlantic should be attempted without a cat onboard. The airship broke the record for a nonstop powered flight at the time by remaining in the air for 711–712 hours, although the crew eventually had to ditch the airship in the Atlantic, only 475 miles (765 km) east of the Maryland coast. Kiddo and the crew were rescued safely by the steamer *Trent* and received a heroes' welcome when they docked in New York City.

In September 2007, a cat called Kattitz somehow managed to escape from his cage en route from Umeå in northern Sweden to Malmö. The cat found himself in the busy Arlanda Airport in Stockholm, where he was able to survive all the hustle and bustle for three weeks. The cat was finally captured after a woman in the control tower noticed a thin, bewildered stray wandering around the airport. Eventually, a hungry Kattitz was lured into a cage again, using cat food. Airport staff then tracked down his owners—a young family in Skåne, southern Sweden, who had been understandably upset when delivered an empty cage at Malmö Airport. When making his second journey, Kattitz was sent home by airplane from Stockholm to Malmö in a more securely sealed carrier cage.

The world's most traveled cat has to be Hamlet, who escaped from his carrier on a flight from Toronto, Canada, at the beginning of 1984. He was found squeezed behind a panel in the hold seven weeks later, by which time he'd flown around 600,000 miles (965,600 km).

In November 2005, Czech Airlines had to fly a cat home on an empty plane after the animal escaped from the cargo hold. Technicians could not find the cat, who was hiding somewhere on the plane. The officials decided it was too dangerous to allow the passengers back onboard if they didn't know the whereabouts of the cat, so the flight from Frankfurt to Prague had to be canceled. Czech Airlines spokeswoman Jitka Novotna said the plane returned to Prague with just the crew and the cat onboard. Once the plane landed, technicians had to dismantle the cargo hold before the cat could finally be removed.

The first stamp featuring a domestic cat dates back to 1930. It's part of a Spanish set of stamps depicting famous aviators of the era. The 1-peseta stamp, commemorating Charles Lindbergh's record-breaking flight from New York to Paris in 1927, showed his cat Patsy wistfully watching his plane take off. The black kitten had accompanied Lindbergh in the cockpit on the first leg of his journey from San Diego to New York. However, the feline did not get to go on the final leg of the flight that made Lindbergh famous.

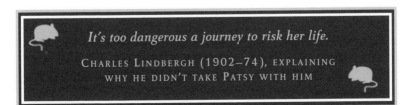

It's too dangerous a journey to risk her life.

CHARLES LINDBERGH (1902–74), EXPLAINING
WHY HE DIDN'T TAKE PATSY WITH HIM

CLEVER CATS

Musicians and scientists were fascinated by Nora, a gray tabby rescue cat who taught herself to play the piano. When she was a year old, Nora climbed up onto the bench in front of a Yamaha Disklavier piano in the middle of the night and began to play, mainly on the D, E, and F keys, but she also included some black keys in her compositions. Nora continued to play the piano regularly and even played duets with her owner and his students. She seemed to like the attention her playing brought her, but she also played when alone.

One summer night in 1955 in Keston, England, Winifred Mansell's pet cat, Ginny, came limping home. Mrs. Mansell removed what she thought to be shards of glass from Ginny's left front paw. On closer examination, the glass proved to be two diamonds worth around $600 apiece.

In April 2006, a cat called Gizmo, who lived with his owners, Nick and Scarlet Sayer, in Santa Clara, California, was fascinated by the way water whirled around a toilet bowl after it was flushed. The smart cat worked out how to create his own entertainment by flushing the toilet himself, using both forepaws to pull down the handle. His toilet-flushing habit first came to light one afternoon when Scarlett was working at home and heard the toilet flush. It puzzled her because she was in the house on her own, but when she went to see what was going on she caught Gizmo leaping up to pull down the handle, then peering over the toilet seat to watch the water swirl away.

Cleo and Tony, two cats from San Jose, California, have a sock fetish. Whenever they are out and about, they bring home someone else's socks: sports socks, brown socks, and some stained green from being dragged through the grass. At first, they brought a sock home only once in a while, then they started bringing socks home everyday and began playing with them. Cleo and Tony's owners tried to find the owners of the socks but nobody has reclaimed any footwear that Cleo and Tony have taken.

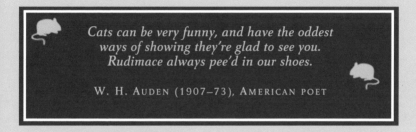

> *Cats can be very funny, and have the oddest*
> *ways of showing they're glad to see you.*
> *Rudimace always pee'd in our shoes.*
>
> W. H. Auden (1907–73), American poet

A cat called Boris nearly managed to order 450 cans of his favorite food on an Internet shopping site while his owner's back was turned. His owner had ordered six cans, but evidently Boris thought that was a little too stingy.

A Chinese man, Mr. Sun, from Beijing, claimed that his two-year-old cat, Agui, could clearly pronounce his own name when he got frightened. He first noticed Agui's linguistic abilities when he was bathing him. The cat was scared of the water, and after a few meows, Mr. Sun was sure he heard a clear "Agui." At first he doubted his own ears, but the cat kept repeating his name in a plaintive childlike voice. After that, whenever Agui was afraid—at the veterinarian or in the bath—he called out "Agui." A video clip of Agui saying his own name while being bathed was filmed at the Fangzhuang Pet Hospital. A hospital spokesperson said hearing his own name over and over again would have made an impression on Agui and it came out under stress.

BEST FRIENDS

Cats are known to make good companions for people, but they seem to also develop special friendships with other animals. In fact, some cats have become seeing-eye cats, not for people, but for other pets in the house. Cats seem to know when one of their furry friends, be it cat or dog, has lost its vision, and they take on the job of guiding the blind animal through life.

One example of a dedicated seeing-eye cat can be found in this story. Mary, an old pug had become completely blind in both eyes. Then one day her owners noticed that their black-and-white rescue kitty, Mancat, was unusually devoted to Mary, always at her side. Then they gradually realized that Mancat was guiding

A speckled cat and a tame hare
Eat at my hearthstone
And sleep there;
And both look up to me alone
For learning and defense
As I look up to Providence.

FROM *TWO SONGS OF A FOOL* BY WILLIAM BUTLER YEATS
(1865–1939), IRISH WRITER

the blind dog around furniture, up the stairs, out into the garden, curling up with her to sleep at night, and even guarding her food bowl so their other dogs wouldn't take advantage of her. Mancat was Mary's self-appointed guide cat for the rest of her life.

🐾 Friendship comes in all sizes. Mr. Chen owned a cat in Jilin, China, and was given a pet mouse by a friend. When the cat first saw the little mouse, it got very excited and circled around and around the cage. After a few days, Mr. Chen let the mouse out of its cage and immediately the cat and the mouse become the best of pals. The cat let the mouse climb all over it and even let it sit on its head. Which only goes to prove that a well-fed domesticated cat does not necessarily see a mouse as food.

🐾 In February 2006, it was reported from Porto Alegre in Brazil that a cat had adopted a bird that was injured when it fell out of its nest and couldn't fly. The cat, known as Chiquita, raised the bird, whose name was Pitico, as if it was its mother. Bird and cat ate from the same plate and the cat even used the injured bird as a decoy to catch other birds—which it did eat.

🐾 All Ball was the pet cat of Koko, the famous gorilla living in Woodside, California, who had been trained to communicate through sign language. In the summer of 1984, Koko asked her trainer, Dr. Francine Patterson, for a cat. Koko selected a gray male Manx from a litter of abandoned kittens and named it All Ball. This particular breed has no tail, and researchers wondered whether that had any bearing on Koko's choice. Koko cared for the kitten as if it were a baby gorilla, until an unfortunate event occurred in December 1984. The curious All Ball escaped from Koko's cage and, sadly, the cat was run over and killed by a car. When Koko found out that All Ball was gone, she was upset and communicated with her trainers using the sign language symbols for cry and sad. In 1985, Koko was allowed to pick out two new kittens from a litter to be her companions. The animals she chose, later named Lipstick and Smokey, were also Manxes.

🐾 A tomcat called Ginger was inseparable from Dante, the winner of the English Derby in 1945. He is just one of several cats that have been invaluable companions to racehorses (see pages 86–87).

CHAPTER 8

Caring for Cats

When you become the custodian of a cat, you effectively strike

a bargain with your feline companion. You pledge to provide a

nourishing diet, fresh water, safe shelter, a hygienic litter box,

frequent grooming, and veterinary care as required. Pay heed to

these welfare essentials, and throw in a warm lap with regular

affectionate stroking, and you stand every chance of developing

a mutually satisfying relationship with a healthy, contented feline

friend, who will live up to its side of the contract by purring and

meowing to your heart's content.

A CAT'S DIET

Cats are strict carnivores. They have to eat meat to live because only meat contains all the essential raw materials to power their chemical factory and ensure their survival.

> The average healthy cat eats about 10¹/₂ ounces (300 g) of meat every day.

A cat doesn't need to eat vegetables because it doesn't get much nutrition out of them. It also doesn't need to eat starchy or sugary foods containing carbohydrates. Although it can utilize carbohydrates as an energy source, it derives most of its energy from fats and proteins.

Because cats have more complex nutritional requirements, they should never be fed the same food as dogs. A cat needs a cocktail of 41 essential nutrients as opposed to the 37 needed by a dog. A good commercial cat food should supply all the nutrients essential to support the feline chemistry.

> The average cat food meal is the equivalent of about five mice.

Americans spend almost $3 billion a year on food for their cats. The United States spends only $700 million on drug prevention and treatment programs.

Cats have a short intestine—it's just long enough to break down protein and fat, which means that they are less able than most animals to digest plant material. However, a small gut has the advantage of keeping them light and lean for leaping and running.

Left to its own devices, a cat selects its food on smell, taste, and texture, often going for foodstuffs containing plenty of meat, with a powerful aroma, a high-fat content, and a mixture of soft and crunchy textures. Generally, cats can't resist very smelly foods, such as sardines and liver.

Most cats like fish, which is a good source of protein. Unfortunately, some types of fish contain an enzyme that destroys the vitamin thiamin. If a cat eats a lot of raw fish, it can develop a thiamin deficiency, which can lead to seizures. However, cooking the fish will deactivate the thiamin-destroying chemical, so it will be safe for your cat. Commercial cat foods contain added thiamin.

> Ideally, a cat's food would be served at about 98°F (36.6°C),
> about the temperature of freshly killed small rodents or birds.

Cats prefer their food at room temperature because they like to be able to smell it. For the cat, serving it straight from the refrigerator would be like eating food when you have a blocked nose—it's tasteless and spoils the appetite.

Unlike humans, cats don't need to eat oranges or other fruit to meet their daily requirement of vitamin C. They can make plenty of their own within their liver.

The cat needs vitamin A for growth, good night vision, and a healthy coat, but it lacks the ability to convert beta-carotenes found in colorful vegetables—such as carrots, tomatoes, sweet potato, spinach, or kale—into retinol, the active form of vitamin A. It has to steal vitamin A that has already been converted from plant sources from good cat food or small mammals that it catches.

The other vital body chemical a cat needs but can't make itself is taurine, an amino acid that is essential for a whole range of bodily functions. The cat depends on obtaining its taurine from meat because it isn't found in plants. In the wild, rodents make up a large part of the feline diet, and rodents have high levels of taurine in their brains. Taurine is added to cat food, but not dog food—which is one of the reasons not to feed your feline the dog's food.

TASTY TIDBITS

🐾 Feeding cats dry foods can help to clean off some of the plaque and calculus buildup on a cat's teeth. A buildup can lead to inflammation of the gums, or gingivitis, which may need dental treatment from a veterinarian. In an ideal world, cats would have their teeth brushed at least once a week, better still every day—but not all cats like the idea of dental hygiene.

🐾 Your cat will prefer eating out of a clean bowl placed in the same quiet spot every day.

🐾 Never put your cat on a starvation diet. Its body will start breaking down its own muscle instead of fat reserves, which can lead to a dangerous buildup of fats in its liver. If a cat won't eat its food for a couple of days, it needs to see a veterinarian.

🐾 Cats may seem like fussy eaters but they actually like change and variety in their diet. Given the choice between bowls of familiar and unfamiliar food, many will go for the unknown. It's just as well there are so many different types of cat food on the supermarket shelves.

> *It has been discovered that the reason your cat declines milk and meat and lets on to live by miraculous intervention is that he catches mice privately.*
>
> MARK TWAIN (1835–1910), WRITING TO HIS DAUGHTER CLARA ABOUT HER BLACK CAT BAMBINO